英译汉基础教程

A BASIC TEXTBOOK FOR ENGLISH-CHINESE TRANSLATION

李冬鹏　李梓铭　关琳　主编

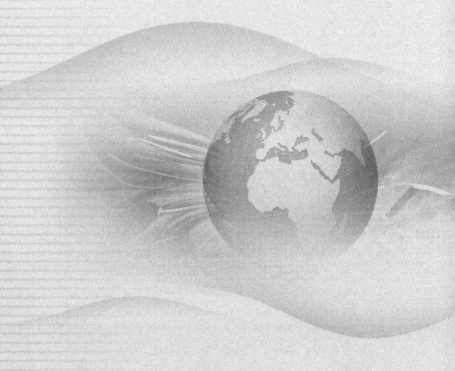

北京理工大学出版社
BEIJING INSTITUTE OF TECHNOLOGY PRESS

版权专有　侵权必究

图书在版编目（CIP）数据

英译汉基础教程 / 李冬鹏，李梓铭，关琳主编 . —北京：北京理工大学出版社，2018.4（2021.7 重印）

ISBN 978-7-5682-5547-9

Ⅰ. ①英… Ⅱ. ①李… ②李… ③关… Ⅲ. ①英语-翻译-高等学校-教材 Ⅳ. ①H315.9

中国版本图书馆 CIP 数据核字（2018）第 070354 号

出版发行 / 北京理工大学出版社有限责任公司

社　　址 / 北京市海淀区中关村南大街 5 号

邮　　编 / 100081

电　　话 /（010）68914775（总编室）
　　　　　（010）82562903（教材售后服务热线）
　　　　　（010）68948351（其他图书服务热线）

网　　址 / http：// www.bitpress.com.cn

经　　销 / 全国各地新华书店

印　　刷 / 北京虎彩文化传播有限公司

开　　本 / 710 毫米×1000 毫米　1/16

印　　张 / 14.75　　　　　　　　　　　　　责任编辑 / 梁铜华

字　　数 / 245 千字　　　　　　　　　　　　文案编辑 / 梁铜华

版　　次 / 2018 年 4 月第 1 版　2021 年 7 月第 3 次印刷　　责任校对 / 杜　枝

定　　价 / 35.00 元　　　　　　　　　　　　责任印制 / 王美丽

图书出现印装质量问题，请拨打售后服务热线，本社负责调换

前　言

本教材是为普通高校英语专业本科生编写的英译汉笔译教材，也可为一般翻译爱好者使用。本教材在编写过程中，主要从以下方面进行了考量：

一、题材方面：本教材尽可能多地选用了近年英文报纸和期刊方面的语料，以保持使用者语言的新鲜性，切实提高其当下工作和学习中所需的翻译能力。

二、体裁方面：本教材在例句、句段、篇章的选择上既涵盖了一般性翻译，还包括文学翻译，以及科技、商务等专门用途英语方面的语料，尽可能与使用者学习、生活和工作中的翻译需求相结合。

三、章节设计方面：本教材每个章节均由技巧讲解、例句翻译、句子英译汉翻译或改错、篇章英译汉翻译四部分组成，各部分相互配合，侧重实践。各章循序渐进，难易结合，形成一个比较完整的英译汉教材体系。此外，本教材在讲解部分和章节练习部分只给原文、原句，有利于培养使用者的独立思考能力，使其真正提高自己的翻译能力。

本教材的编写者均在全日制高等学校任教，口笔译教学和实践经验较为丰富。本教材系编者多年教学经验和研究的一些总结，希望同广大同行进行交流，对英译汉笔译教学做更深入的研究和探讨。本教材所用例句和篇章大部分出自参考文献中所列出的书刊和网络资料，由于篇幅有限，恕不一一标明出处。

本教材多人执笔，再加上作者水平有限，肤浅之处和错误之处在所难免，恳请广大读者批评指正。

编　者
2018 年 1 月

目 录

第1章 西方翻译史简介 ···································· 1
 第1节 中西译学界对翻译史的不同划分 ···························· 2
 第2节 西方翻译史的三个阶段 ······································ 5

第2章 翻译概述 ·· 16
 第1节 翻译的定义 ·· 17
 第2节 翻译的类别 ·· 19
 第3节 翻译标准 ·· 20
 第4节 翻译的过程 ·· 22
 第5节 译者的素质 ·· 23

第3章 英汉语言对比 ·· 24
 第1节 英汉语言宏观对比 ·· 25
 第2节 英汉语言微观对比 ·· 31

第4章 直译与意译 ·· 42
 第1节 直译法 ·· 43
 第2节 意译法 ·· 45
 第3节 直译与意译相结合 ·· 47

第5章 词义的选择与引申 ·· 51
 第1节 词义的选择 ·· 52
 第2节 词义的褒贬 ·· 56
 第3节 词义的轻重 ·· 58
 第4节 词义的引申 ·· 59

第6章 转译法 ·· 64
 第1节 转译为动词 ·· 65
 第2节 转译为名词 ·· 69
 第3节 其他词类间的转译 ·· 71

第7章 增词法 ····· 75
- 第1节 语法上的增补 ····· 76
- 第2节 语义上的增补 ····· 80
- 第3节 修辞上的增补 ····· 85
- 第4节 文化背景增补 ····· 86

第8章 减词法 ····· 90
- 第1节 语法上的减省 ····· 91
- 第2节 修辞上的减省 ····· 97

第9章 正反译法 ····· 101
- 第1节 正说反译 ····· 102
- 第2节 反说正译 ····· 105
- 第3节 双重否定句 ····· 106
- 第4节 否定陷阱 ····· 108

第10章 语序调整 ····· 114
- 第1节 词序调整 ····· 115
- 第2节 句序调整 ····· 116

第11章 分译法 ····· 122
- 第1节 单词的分译 ····· 123
- 第2节 短语的分译 ····· 124
- 第3节 句子的分译 ····· 127

第12章 合译法 ····· 131
- 第1节 单词的合译 ····· 132
- 第2节 句子的合译 ····· 133

第13章 被动句的翻译 ····· 138
- 第1节 带施动者的被动句 ····· 140
- 第2节 不带施动者的被动句 ····· 142

第14章 定语从句 ····· 148
- 第1节 合译法 ····· 149
- 第2节 分译法 ····· 152
- 第3节 转译法 ····· 155

第15章 状语从句 ····· 160
- 第1节 时间状语从句 ····· 161

第 2 节 地点状语从句 ……………………………………… 163
第 3 节 原因状语从句 ……………………………………… 164
第 4 节 条件状语从句 ……………………………………… 165
第 5 节 让步状语从句 ……………………………………… 166
第 6 节 目的状语从句 ……………………………………… 167
第 7 节 结果状语从句 ……………………………………… 168
第 8 节 方式状语从句 ……………………………………… 169

第 16 章 名词性从句 ……………………………………………… 172
第 1 节 主语从句 …………………………………………… 173
第 2 节 宾语从句 …………………………………………… 175
第 3 节 表语从句 …………………………………………… 177
第 4 节 同位语从句 ………………………………………… 178

附录一 英译汉篇章练习 ………………………………………… 183
附录二 英译汉篇章练习答案 …………………………………… 204
参考文献 …………………………………………………………… 220

第1章

西方翻译史简介

翻译活动因受到政治、经济、文化、宗教、语言等多种因素的影响,并不完全随着社会时代的更替而立即发生变化。它的变化往往是跨越历史时代的。在译学界,国内外专家、学者根据不同的标准和原则,对西方翻译史做了不同的划分。

第1节　中西译学界对翻译史的不同划分

从严格意义上说，西方的第一部译作是在约公元前3世纪中叶由安德罗尼柯用拉丁语翻译的希腊荷马史诗《奥德赛》。对这两千多年翻译史的分期，人们因视角不同、所持的划分标准不同，观点颇不一致，至今并无统一的结论。

廖七一援引历史学者的三分法，着重翻译理论思想的演变，采用轻历史划分、重翻译思想界定，薄古厚今的原则，将西方翻译理论的发展大致分为三大时期：(1) 古典译论时期，公元前3—18世纪；(2) 近代译论时期，18世纪末—20世纪初；(3) 当代译论时期，20世纪初至今。

潘文国则强调学科概念，以是否具有学科意识为依据，同样把西方翻译研究史分为三个阶段：(1) 从古代的西塞罗（Cicero）到1959年，称作传统的翻译学阶段；(2) 从1959年雅各布逊（Jacobson）发表《翻译的语言观》开始到1972年，称作现代的翻译学阶段；(3) 从1972年霍尔姆斯（Holmes）发表《翻译研究的名与实》开始至今为当代的翻译学阶段。

谭载喜更关注历史因素对翻译事业的影响，他把西方翻译史划分为六个时期：(1) 发轫于公元前4世纪的肇始阶段；(2) 罗马帝国的后期至中世纪；(3) 中世纪时期；(4) 文艺复兴时期；(5) 近代翻译时期，即17—20世纪上半叶；(6) 第二次世界大战结束至今。

奈达（Nida）根据翻译思想的发展，把西方翻译史划分为四个时期：(1) 语文学翻译；(2) 语言学翻译；(3) 交际学翻译；(4) 社会符号学翻译。他把20世纪50年代以前的翻译思想视作一个整体，从而与具有现代翻译思想的当代翻译作出区分。

斯坦纳（Steiner）认为西方翻译理论的研究大体经历了四个时期：(1) 古典译论至18世纪末泰特勒和坎贝尔翻译"三原则"的发表，这一时期翻译论述及理论直接来自翻译实践；(2) 从施莱尔马赫至20世纪中叶，通过理论研究和阐释研究发展了翻译研究术语及方法；(3) "二战"结束至20世纪70年代，以翻译语言学派的兴起为标志，将结构主义语言学和交际理论引入翻译研究；(4) 20世纪70年代至今，新兴学派林立，跨学科研究蓬勃发展。

巴斯奈特（Bassnett）认为不同时期有不同的翻译观，更合适的做法是以翻译观念为依据来进行划分：(1) 罗马时期的翻译，是为了丰富本国的文学系统，强调译作的美学标准，而不关注是否忠实；(2) 《圣经》翻译，是作为教义的武器、作为政治冲突的武器，译者既有美学的标准，也有福音传教士的标准；(3) 教育与通俗语言时期，强调《圣经》翻译的教育功能，以大家都能够懂的语言来翻译；(4) 早期的理论家，由于印刷术的发明、新大陆的发现影响了社会文化观念，同样影响了翻译功能的改变，形成了较为严谨的翻译理论；(5) 文艺复兴时期，翻译是国家大事、宗教大事，译者是革命的活动者，不再是屈从于作者或原文的奴仆；(6) 17世纪的翻译，作家为了寻求新的创作模式而翻译、模仿希腊的作品，译者与作者地位平等；(7) 18世纪的翻译，译者关注翻译的道德问题，关注再创原作精神的问题；(8) 浪漫主义时期的翻译，肯定译者个人的创造力；(9) 后浪漫主义时期的翻译，译者屈从于原作的形式与语言，尽可能保留原作的特殊性；(10) 维多利亚时期的翻译，开始贬低翻译，不再把它看作丰富本国文化的手段；(11) 使用古词，采取复古的原则，认为翻译应该恢复原作；(12) 20世纪的翻译，成为独立的研究对象。巴斯奈特认为，不要局限于狭隘的、固定的角度来研究翻译，而是要采取系统的、历时性的方法研究翻译。巴斯奈特的划分颇具其个人特色，只是这种过细的划分，容易给人一种琐碎的感觉，不易看到整体的翻译史。

道勒拉普（Dollerup）把欧洲翻译史划分为六个阶段：(1) 圣经翻译阶段（1530年以前）；(2) 路德宗教改革到法国大革命时期（1530—1790年），民族文学增长，翻译更加自由；(3) 法国大革命到"二战"时期（1789—1940年），教育的普及、工业革命导致的贸易增长等因素促进翻译的繁荣，翻译成为一种职业，翻译的标准不断改进；(4) 殖民解体到冷战阶段（1945—1970年），技术、商业和科技翻译成为主流，译者的地位和可见性显著提高；(5) 欧盟扩张到冷战结束（1970—1990年），经过正式培训的译员加入翻译行业，翻译团体和翻译组织机构成立，翻译成为一门新的学科；(6) 新时期的翻译（1990年至现在），各民族间的翻译量增长，电子工具、翻译记忆、网络等工具运用于翻译。他的划分比较偏重20世纪欧洲翻译史的发展轨迹，但对整体的西方翻译史的发展似乎不是那么关注。

人类在《圣经》翻译之前的翻译活动，还处在翻译的摸索阶段，严格而言，还谈不上有什么理论认识，至多也仅是对翻译的一些朦胧感知而已。从公元前250年左右《七十子希腊文本》的翻译活动开始，一直持续到16世纪的《圣经》翻译，这段时期我们把它命名为宗教典籍翻译阶段，这一阶段对翻译的探讨确立了人类关于翻译的基本理念，包括最基本的翻译方法论，如直译、意译、可译、不可译等问题。随着民族语言与民族文学的确立，尤其是西方文艺复兴运动兴起之后，文学翻译开始成为翻译的主流，从而开启了以文学名著、社科经典为主要翻译对象的文学翻译阶段。在这一阶段，对翻译的理论探讨更加丰富和深入，并且产生了针对各种文学类别、体裁作品的翻译理论。第二次世界大战以后，实用性质的非文学翻译（即实用文献的翻译）占据了翻译生产的主流，翻译发展为一个专门的职业，翻译理论意识空前高涨，翻译学科得到快速成长，由此开始了人类翻译发展史的第三阶段——实用文献翻译阶段。当然，有必要说明的是，我们对人类翻译发展史的这种三阶段划分，依据的是每一阶段的主流翻译对象，但它们之间是相互交叉的，而并不是说一个阶段只有一种翻译对象。同理，对翻译的观念也是相互交叉的，即使在目前的实用文献翻译阶段，文学翻译或宗教翻译阶段所形成的译学理念和理论仍然在发挥作用和影响，只是与实用文献的翻译相比，它们在整个翻译活动和翻译产业中所占的比例比从前要小，正在边缘化，其影响也正在日渐缩小。

第 2 节　西方翻译史的三个阶段

翻译史的分期不能机械地按照人类社会历史的分期来划分，而应当按翻译活动自身的发展规律来划分；同时，还需要特别强调的是，这种划分应该有助于揭示翻译发展史的本质，有助于认识和把握翻译活动的发展脉络和主要翻译理念的演变，有助于认识当前翻译活动在整个翻译史上的历史定位。为此，我们主要依据历史上主流翻译对象的变化，结合人类对翻译活动认识的发展以及翻译在各历史阶段的社会中所占据的地位和影响，尝试把西方翻译发展史划分为三个不同的阶段，即以宗教文献为主要翻译对象的宗教典籍翻译阶段、以文学（也包括一定的社科）经典名著为主要翻译对象的文学翻译阶段和以实用文献为主要翻译对象的非文学翻译阶段。宗教翻译奠定了人类对翻译的最基本的认识基础，确立了翻译的基本理念；文学翻译丰富、深化了人类关于翻译的基本理念，而实用文献的翻译则把翻译带入了职业翻译时代，为传统的翻译理念注入了新的、不同于建立在宗教文献翻译和文学翻译基础上的翻译理念，同时也促进了当代翻译事业的进一步繁荣。

2.1　宗教典籍（《圣经》）翻译阶段

西方的宗教典籍翻译阶段的主要翻译对象就是《圣经》，包括讲述历史、预言、诗歌和神学的 66 部书，历时 1 600 年的创作，至少由 40 位不同的作者写成。《圣经·旧约》包含 39 部书，写于前 1500—前 400 年。除了一小部分以外，主要用希伯来文写成。《圣经·新约》包含 27 本书，在 40—90 年写成。《圣经》翻译历时 2 200 多年，经历了几个里程碑式的阶段：首先是公元前的《七十子希腊文本》；其次是 4—5 世纪的《通俗拉丁文本圣经》；之后是中世纪初期各民族语的古文本（如古德语译本、古法语译本）、16 世纪宗教改革运动以来的近代文本（如德国的路德本、西班牙的卡西欧多罗本、英国的钦定本、俄罗斯的尼康本），以及各式各样的现代文本（如英语的《美国标准本圣经》、《新英语圣经》和《今日英语文本》等）。

《七十子希腊文本》是对犹太《圣经》希腊文翻译的称呼。该译本起源于埃及的亚历山大大帝，是在前 285—前 249 年翻译完成的。它在希腊的犹太人中被广泛使用，因为遍及整个帝国的犹太人开始逐渐忘记他们的希伯来语言，所以把希伯来文翻译成了希腊文。这也让许多非犹太人有了机会了解犹太教。《七十子希腊文本》一直被奉为经典译本，成了"第二原本"。直到今天，东正教会对《圣经·旧约》的教导仍然依靠希腊文译本。一些现代《圣经》翻译也用希腊文译本跟希伯来文原稿一起作为翻译的源本。古拉丁语、斯拉夫语和阿拉伯语等语言中的许多《圣经》译文则不以希伯来原文而以希腊语译文为源本。

在较早时期就有人将《圣经》译成拉丁语，到4世纪这一翻译活动达到了高潮，其结果就是出现了各式各样的译本。哲罗姆（Jerome）于382—405年翻译的《通俗拉丁文本圣经》成为钦定本，标志着《圣经》翻译取得了与世俗文学翻译分庭抗礼的重要地位，在以后的较长时间里超过了世俗文学的翻译而成为西方翻译的主流。由于发现希伯来文与希腊文译本之间存在着若干歧义，所以于382年，哲罗姆应教皇达马苏一世（Pope Damasus Ⅰ）之请将《圣经》译成拉丁文。他历时23年，将已有的旧拉丁文版本比对希伯来文《圣经》，经过翻译整理之后，最终完成了《通俗拉丁文本圣经》。《通俗拉丁文本圣经》到了16世纪时的"特兰托会议"（Council of Trent，1546年）才正式成为官方版本。这个译本很成功，成为罗马天主教所承认的唯一文本，也成为后来阿尔弗雷德国王（King Alfred）所参考的版本。

从罗马帝国时代到中世纪初期，教会在教育、哲学、文化以至整个精神领域里占有绝对的统治地位，因此《圣经》和其他宗教作品的诠释和翻译得到了进一步加强。他们为了传教，开始用德语口头翻译宗教文献，800年前后出现了第一部德译本《圣经》，该译本也被称为德语最早的文字。

中世纪末期，随着欧洲各民族国家的建立，民族地域逐渐划定，民族要求日趋强烈，民族语言也相继形成。因此，用民族语言从事较大规模的翻译到中世纪末期开始出现，有的译本甚至成为该民族语言的第一批文学材料。宗教改革家马丁·路德（Martin Luther，1483—1546年）顺从民众的意愿，采用民众的语言，于1522—1534年翻译刊行第一部"民众的圣经"，使任何识字的人都有可能亲自学习《圣经》，而不依赖教会及其教士，开创了现代德语发展的新纪元。1611年《钦定本圣经》的翻译出版则标志着英国翻译史上又一次大发展。之所以称它为"钦定"，是指这个译本得到英国国王詹姆士一世（James Ⅰ）的指令，由47名学者于1607年开始翻译，用它代替以前所用的英译本，用于礼拜时的诵读。《钦定本圣经》文体优美，朗读时铿锵有力，颇有韵味，具有较强的文学性。随着文艺复兴运动的兴起，民族主义在政治上抬头，教会的力量相对减弱，《圣经》翻译的热情慢慢消退。尽管如此，《圣经》在今天仍然是世界上翻译语种最多的书籍，始终吸引着翻译家与学者们的兴趣。

《圣经》翻译家对翻译的认识，大多是对自身翻译经验的总结，对翻译方法的总结，从字对字的直译，到随意性极大的意译，再由较成熟的直译到较成熟的意译，并最终实现直译与意译的调和；最初以词为翻译单位逐渐依次转变为以句子、话语为翻译单位。《圣经》翻译最初坚持直译的主要原因还是"宗教经典神圣不可侵犯"，正如斐洛（Philo, 20 B. C.—A. D. 50）所认为的，《圣经》翻译是神圣的，译者单凭精通两种语言而无"上帝的感召"，是不能从事翻译的。为了避免在翻译中的主观随意，译者就只好在词序和措辞等方面采取死译，译者的任务是做到字字对译，丝毫不必顾及译语中的特殊形式和习惯。这种字对字的直译，其译文很难为普通大众所理解。但随着译者语言水平的提高和翻译经验的积累，译者跳出了逐字对译的藩篱，而注重意义的整体传达，但并不绝对排除直译的方法。哲罗姆认识到译者的选词造句不是靠"上帝的感召"，而是靠译者本人的博识和对语言的精通来实现的，而且各种语言在用词风格、表达习惯、句法及语义、内容等方面都有区别，因而翻译中只能采用意译的方法。后来《圣经》的解释权收归到少数神甫手中，"翻译必须依靠上帝感召"的认识再次抬头，强调只有受了"上帝的感召"的人才有资格翻译《圣经》。但是，随着民族国家的逐步形成，各民族自我意识的进一步加强，民族语言的地位得到了提高，《圣经》翻译也转而以各民族语为主。在翻译《圣经》的过程中，只要不违背原意，则不必拘泥于原文形式，因为翻译的目的是满足普通大众的需求，并不是为少数研究者而译。《圣经》翻译重在正确传达意义，让读者理解。

2.2 文学翻译阶段

西方各国（主要指西欧，特别是英国、法国与德国）在历史、社会、宗教、文化以及文学方面有着极其密切的关系，从文艺复兴开始的各种文学运动和风格都远远超越了一个国家的边界，其文学的发展过程有明显的相似性，甚至文学中体裁和风格的更替也都反映出类似的序列关系，而这一切的变化无不与文学翻译有着密切的关系。完全按照国别或时间来切割西方的文学翻译活动与翻译理念的发展，很容易顾此失彼。因此，为了突出文学翻译与文学创作之间的相互影响，并揭示翻译理论思想的演进过程，我们把西方的文学翻译划分为四个时期，即早期的文学翻译（民族语言的形成到文艺复兴时期）、启蒙时期的文学翻译（17—18世纪）、浪漫主义时期的文学翻译（18世纪末—19世纪三四十年代）、现代主义时期的文学翻译（19世纪末—"二战"结束）。

2.2.1 西方早期的文学翻译

西方早期的文学翻译，是使用本民族语言进行文学创作的"副产品"，同民族语言的形成与民族文学自身的发展密切相关。在翻译理论方面，主要是围绕直译与意译的讨论，以及如何使用民族语言来摆脱拉丁语的影响。

本民族语言的成熟与民族文学的发展，是文学翻译存在的前提。到了16世纪文艺复兴时期，法国文学翻译依然只是创作之余的"副产品"，翻译质量不高，影响也不大。贡献最为突出的是雅克·阿米欧（Jacques Amyot, 1513—1593年），他先后用了17年时间（1542—1559年）译出了普鲁塔克（Plutarch）的《希腊罗马名人比较列传》（简称《名人传》，*Life of Noble Grecians and Romans*）。阿米欧采用了创造性意译，从而把原作变成了他自己的《名人传》。他的译本获得了成功，给同时代和后来的法国以及西欧其他国家的作家提供了创作素材。阿米欧的翻译强调兼顾内容与形式，遵循直译与意译的统一，把大众的语言与学者的语言熔于一炉，并创造了大量新词，极大地丰富了法语的词汇。

文艺复兴在英国是以重新发现希腊、罗马的古典文化开始的。大学里恢复了古希腊语的教学，接着出现了规模宏大的翻译活动，众多学者、作家将古代希腊、罗马和近代意、法等国的学术和文学名著译成了早期近代英语。整个伊丽莎白一世时期英国最著名的译作就是托马斯·诺斯爵士（Sir Thomas North, 1535—1604年）于1579年从阿米欧的法语版转译而成的《名人传》。诺斯的翻译不同于法语的风格，如用词的改动、精神实质的修改，均是在原作基础上的一种创作。诺斯译笔优雅地道，人们常把他的译本误认为原作，他的译作也为莎士比亚创作罗马悲剧提供了素材。1603年，弗罗里欧（Florio, 1553—1625年?）把欧洲散文的创始者法国思想家蒙田（Montaigne）的《随笔集》翻译为英语，成为英语文学翻译中的经典。

2.2.2 启蒙时期的文学翻译

启蒙运动是17—18世纪继文艺复兴之后欧洲发生的又一次思想解放运动。以城市中产阶级为主的文学作品的读者群体逐渐形成，再加上杂志的推波助澜以及出版翻译作品所带来的经济利益，这些都使文学翻译迅速繁荣起来。

17世纪英国最伟大的翻译家是约翰·德莱顿（John Dryden, 1631—1700年），他翻译过普鲁塔克的《希腊罗马名人比较列传》以及薄伽丘、奥维德、贺拉斯、荷马等人的作品。他的翻译风格因所译作品风格的不同而不同，文字平易流畅。在翻译理论方面，他写过大量的论文和序言，阐述自己的观点，明确而系统地提出了翻译的原则。德莱顿的翻译原则与观点主要有以下几个方面：（1）翻译是艺术；（2）翻译必须掌握原作特征；（3）翻译必须考虑读者；（4）译者必须绝对服从原作的意思；（5）翻译可以借用外来词；（6）翻译分为三类，即词译（或逐词译，metaphrase）、释译（paraphrase）、拟译（imitation）。他主张采取折中的方式，即介于过分随便与过分呆板之间的释译。

英国 18 世纪的翻译家亚历山大·蒲柏（Alexander Pope，1688—1744 年）翻译了《伊利亚特》（6 卷）和《奥德赛》（5 卷）。与他的创作一样，其翻译采取的是英国读者熟悉的双韵史诗体，译文用词隽永，风格清雅，在相当长的时间里被读者奉为标准英译本。为了满足当代读者的需求，他大量使用 18 世纪英诗创作中惯用的词汇，因此在某种程度上蒲柏的译作变成了他本人的创作。在译作的序言中蒲柏指出，好的翻译采取直译肯定行不通，用草率的拟译法来取代直译以弥补它的缺陷，也同样是一大错误。译者必须在最大程度上忠实原作，而不应当企图超过原作者。

17 世纪末法国的"古今之争"标志着古典主义的没落和启蒙文学的开始。一些翻译家厚今薄古，任意发挥，较为典型的是阿布朗古尔（Ablancourt，1606—1664 年），其译作被称作"美而不忠的翻译"。他的翻译往往根据原作的大意，不管原来的风格如何，只要译文具有文学性和可读性，能使当代读者爱看，就不惜牺牲一切任意增删内容，能修改就修改，能发挥就发挥，丝毫不顾及译文的准确性。这样的翻译遭到了一些人的反对，但 17 世纪翻译的主流还是不准确的翻译，翻译家都竭力从理论上对自己采取的方法加以解释和辩护。

法国 18 世纪的启蒙运动文学家多数以思想家的身份出现，文学作品只是表达思想的一种辅助手段。尽管法国启蒙思想家依照古典艺术法则对莎士比亚的评价并不高，但莎士比亚作品的译介依然是 18 世纪法国文学翻译最主要的内容。初期的翻译家翻译莎士比亚的戏剧时，为了使译文符合法国的高雅文体，不惜删改原作。真正认识到莎士比亚独特写作风格的翻译家是皮埃尔·勒图尔纳（Pierre le Touneur，1736—1788 年），他翻译了《莎士比亚全集》，其风格为后来莎士比亚作品的翻译树立了榜样。他强调忠实原作，要完整地保留原作的精神实质，不赞成删改原文以迎合法国人崇尚典雅的口味，而主张保留原作生动的形象和通俗的语言风格。

德国的启蒙运动是在先进的英国和法国的影响下兴起的。德国"巴洛克诗歌之父"马丁·奥皮茨（Martin Opitz，1597—1639 年）翻译引进了古希腊、罗马的颂歌体以及意大利、法国的十四行诗。17 世纪，西欧的长篇小说，特别是西班牙的骑士冒险小说和英国的田园牧歌小说，被译介到了德国，成了德国文坛模仿的对象。

2.2.3 浪漫主义时期的文学翻译

浪漫主义时期的翻译家和翻译理论家大多是当时的著名作家，所以该时期的翻译理论无不受到浪漫主义文学思想的影响。这一时期翻译的重心从古代作品转移到近代作品或当代作品；与此同时，文学翻译的基本问题也都得到了深入的探讨，且表现出系统性、理论性的特点。英国翻译理论家亚历山大·弗雷泽·泰特勒（Alexander Fraser Tytler，1747—1814年）于1792年出版的《论翻译的原则》代表了这一时期翻译理论的最高成就。泰特勒认为出色的翻译应该是将原文的优点完整无缺地以另一种语言表达出来，使译文读者对译文理解得如原文读者般清楚透彻，感受也像原文读者一样深切强烈。在此基础上，他提出了著名的"翻译三原则"：（1）译者应精通原作语言和题材，完全再现原作的思想；（2）译者应准确判断和鉴赏原作的风格，并想象原作者如果用译语创作该如何表现自己，以使译作的风格、手法与原作等同；（3）译作应与原作同样通顺。

德国浪漫主义时期的著名作家几乎个个都是翻译的好手，他们翻译了大量古希腊、罗马和近代以来英、法、西班牙等国的作品。这些作家兼翻译家在理论上亦多有阐发，从文学及语言学的角度，对翻译进行了多层次的探讨，使德国成为欧洲翻译理论研究的中心。

维兰德（Wieland，1733—1813年）于1762—1766年翻译出版了8册莎士比亚的作品，埃申堡（Eschenburg，1743—1820年）在1775—1782年用散文的形式翻译了莎士比亚的作品。这些散文译本通俗易懂，流传很快，影响深远。歌德甚至认为德国人对莎士比亚的赏识恐怕连英国人也有所不及。蒂克（Tieck，1773—1853年）、施莱格尔（Schlegel，1767—1845年）等也翻译了莎士比亚的作品。

施莱尔马赫（Schleiermacher，1768—1834年）1813年的《论翻译的方法》是浪漫主义时期最主要的翻译理论文献，其主要观点是：（1）翻译分笔译和口译；（2）翻译分真正的翻译和机械的翻译，文学作品和自然科学的笔译属于真正的翻译，实用性的口译属于机械的翻译；（3）翻译必须正确理解语言与思维的辩证关系；（4）翻译可有两种途径：一是尽量不打扰作者而将读者移近作者；二是尽量不打扰读者而将作者移近读者。施莱尔马赫认为，如果要获得完美的翻译，译者应该努力将自己从作品中获得的同样的意象、印象，原原本本、不偏不倚地传递给读者，因此他千方百计地将读者引向他自己的观点。

歌德（Goethe，1749—1832年）认为，翻译不是完美的，但仍是最重要、最有价值的活动之一，译者是"人民的先知"。他甚至认为译者铸造了一种完全适合于交流两国思想的语言，其潜台词是翻译对译入国语言的形成和发展有相当的影响；不同语言表达的意思具有共性，文学是可译的；最恰当的翻译是朴实无华的翻译，译诗的最好方法是采用散文体。他把翻译分为三类：传递知识的翻译（informative translation）、按照译语文化规范的改编性翻译（adaptation）、逐行对照翻译（interlinear translation）。他最为推崇第三种翻译，认为这样的翻译使原文与译文共生、译语和源语融合为一，产生了新的形式，而又没有抛弃各自原有的成分。

荷尔德林（Hoelderlin，1770—1843年）认为人类每一种具体语言都是同一基本语言（纯语言）的体现，翻译就是寻找构成这一基本语言的核心成分即意思。荷尔德林把对语言的理解和复述过程当成对直觉进行考古研究的过程。他主张采取逐字对译，在源语和目标语之间开辟一个中间地带，探寻人类语言所共有的东西。

以德国为代表的西方译界在当时多主张异化翻译，翻译家和作家认识到其他语言并不比自己的母语低下，也正是这种语言观念的转变，使得翻译家开始采取平等的态度对待原文。翻译开始容忍文化的差异，翻译只能试探性地接近原文，鼓励向原文靠近。

2.2.4 现代主义时期的文学翻译

英国文学评论家康诺利（Connolly）在1965年出版了《现代主义运动——1880—1950年英、法、美现代主义代表作一百种》，其标题指明了现代主义的上限和下限。英国、法国、德国等国先后进入了帝国主义时期，各国坚持强硬的民族主义路线，对本民族文化的自豪感增强，不再把翻译看作丰富民族文化的主要手段，并进而贬低翻译的作用。西方各国除了相互翻译各国的现、当代文学作品外，还把目光投向了殖民地国家和东方各国的文学经典作品。在翻译理论方面，受现代主义文学思想的影响，对传统的翻译理论也提出了深刻的反省，特别是对语言的普遍性提出了质疑，原作的意义变得隐晦难解，译者必须根据自己的体验去填补文本的空白。所以，这一时期的翻译理论，更加注重翻译的创造性，更加关注翻译中的语言问题，虽没有脱离译文选词造句等翻译技巧的论述，但为翻译研究的语言学转向奠定了基础，为把翻译文学看作独立的存在提供了理论思考。

英国作家爱德华·菲茨杰拉德（Edward Fitzgerald，1809—1883年）翻译波斯诗人莪默·伽亚谟（Omar Khayyam）的《鲁拜集》时，认为译者所要做的是如何把粗糙得像黏土一样的原作塑造成受人欢迎的作品，提升原作的档次。这时期的译者对殖民地国家的作品随意改写，却不敢对荷马、维吉尔等人的作品肆意妄为。这种典型的民族主义翻译观遭到后殖民翻译学者的揭露与抵制，翻译在殖民化过程中扮演了不太光彩的角色。

波斯盖特（Postgate，1853—1926年）是英国著名的文学家、翻译家、翻译理论家。在《译论与译作》中，他提出了前瞻式翻译（prospective translation）和后顾式翻译（retrospective translation）。前瞻式翻译是指译者心中始终装着读者，采用自由的方法，使用常见的表达形式，以保证读者原有的思想不受冲击及其预测不受干扰，翻译的目的是要表现译者精通译文语言，重点在于译文而不在原文。后顾式翻译是指译者总是着眼于原作者，因为翻译的目的是传授原文知识，而不是向前观看、考虑译作的读者。

法国文学的优良传统是善于通过翻译吸收外来文化。19世纪下半叶，法国将异军突起的俄国小说大量译介为法语。在翻译理论方面，马鲁佐（Marouzeau，1878—1964年）的《论拉丁语的翻译》是法语中一篇重要的翻译理论文献。他认为翻译是一门技巧，译者应向读者揭示原作的内容，而不是它的外壳；要使用活的语言，假设原作者现在还活着，他会用什么方式来表达同一事物。

在翻译理论方面，德国影响最大的是著名思想家瓦尔特·本雅明（Walter Benjamin，1892—1940年）。他于1914年开始翻译波德莱尔（Baudelaire）的诗，并在之后翻译出版了波德莱尔的诗集《巴黎风光》。本雅明在该书的译序《译者的任务》中并没有直接论及波德莱尔或他的这部诗集，而是论述了他对原作、翻译与"纯语言"的关系的思考。对本雅明而言，译者的任务就是弥合语言的碎片，回归到语言堕落之前的整体和谐状态。平庸译者对原作意义的关注远远多于对其文学性和语言风格的关注，他们只知译作的存在是为了服务于原作，只能译出原作中非本质的内容。本雅明指出，译作虽以原作为依据，但是原作的来世是原作生命的延续，译作不必追求与原作意义相仿，译者的任务就是要用自己的语言去释放被另一种语言的咒符困住的纯语言，就是要在对原作的再创造中解放那种被囚禁的语言。真正的译作是透明的，它不会掩盖原作，不会遮蔽原作的光芒，所以他主张双语隔行对照式样是一切翻译的范本。当代美国翻译理论家根茨勒（Gentzler）认为，英美解构主义者有关翻译问题的讨论，主要是围绕对本雅明的《译者的任务》一文的评论展开的。《译者的任务》也因此被誉为翻译理论的"圣经"、解构主义翻译理论的经典。

俄国在18世纪初进入彼得大帝时代，文学翻译特别是法国文学翻译的作品显著增多，在俄国兴起了法国热，俄国第一位大学者、诗人、语言学家和翻译家米哈伊尔·罗蒙诺索夫（Mikhil Lomonosov，1711—1765年）改造了那些进入俄语中的外来词，使其俄国化。由于翻译被看作一种创造性活动，所以自由翻译颇为盛行，以至于出现为适应俄国口味而随意改动原作的现象。这种自由翻译观一直持续到19世纪。19世纪俄国最伟大的诗人普希金（Pushkin，1799—1837年）根据自身的文学翻译实践，发表了为数不多的翻译评论，推动了俄国的文学翻译活动。他认为，译者选材应有自己的主张，在处理原作时应有充分的自由，但原作的独特之处应尽量保留。自普希金开始，后来的一些著名诗人、作家也都对翻译问题发表了不少自己的见解，并指出翻译时应注意作品的思想内容和文学价值以及译作内容与形式的统一、强调翻译应该为读者服务、注意译文的人民性，等等。进入苏联时期，翻译为人民服务、为社会主义服务成为评价一切翻译作品的重要标准；外国文学作品的翻译更加有组织、有计划、有系统；翻译选题严格按照原作的思想性、艺术性和知识价值来确定；苏联国内各民族语言之间的翻译更是得到了极大的发展；译界普遍遵循忠实、准确的翻译原则。

"二战"之后，文学翻译虽然逐渐不再占据主流，但对文学翻译的研究却取得了明显的突破。20世纪70年代之后，以色列、荷兰、比利时等国家的学者把翻译文学看作一种相对独立的存在，看到了文学翻译对本土文学创作的巨大影响。他们认为翻译文学可以在目标语文学的多元系统中占据中心位置，成为最活跃的系统，是民族文学的一个组成部分。这种认识使文学翻译家及其作品（译作）的作用得到了真正的认可，是文学翻译理论的一个重大突破。

2.3 非文学（实用文献）翻译阶段

第二次世界大战结束以来，出于实际需要，商业、外交、科技方面的翻译蓬勃兴起，其声势日渐超过文学翻译，成为西方现代翻译发展的一项主要内容。非文学翻译的繁荣体现在翻译从业者的职业化、翻译行业的产业化、翻译观念的现代化、翻译研究的学科化等方面。"二战"之后，各种国际组织成立，对职业翻译的需求激增。从纽伦堡大审判，到联合国的成立，到欧洲经济共同体以及各种区域性组织、国际行业组织的成立等，都需要大量的职业翻译人员来保障各主体国家和地区能够以母语来阐明各自的立场。职业翻译还体现在国家层面的需求，一些多语言、多文化的国家用法律的形式规定了多种官方语言，从而保障了翻译职业的稳定需求。各类专门翻译院系的成立、翻译培训的专门化，保证了翻译从业者的职业素养。翻译职业的资质认证为翻译职业化提供了标准和壁垒。翻译发展为一种由千万人参与、内容涉及各个领域的专门职业。

实用文献翻译的繁荣，主要得益于以信息技术为核心的第三次科技革命，以及涵盖政治、经济、科技、文化、媒体、生态和社会认同等方面的全球化发展。经济的全球化带动了资本、商品、技术、劳动力在全球范围内日益频繁的流动，不同文化跨越民族范围的接触交流以及相互吸收融合，都为翻译创造了前所未有的巨大市场。国际贸易的增长、国际组织的壮大、各个国家之间文化交流的加深以及软件产业所促成的本地化需求，使翻译变成了社会生活不可或缺的一部分，并发展为一个独立的产业。

由此可见，文学翻译已经只是当前所有实际翻译活动中很小的一部分，文学翻译的边缘化、非主流化是一个不可回避的事实，而科技、商业、娱乐、媒体等实用文献的翻译越来越成为当今翻译的主流。诸如要旨翻译、现场翻译、视译、配音、字幕翻译、唱词字幕翻译等，还有翻译版权问题、已有翻译的重复使用问题等，都是文学翻译所忽略的领域。翻译的社会维度，不仅涉及翻译规范，还包括其他传播与接受翻译的代理人与机构，如发送者、客户、校订者、其他译者、出版社、公司等，因此，它会在翻译产业化过程中面临新问题。对这些问题的关注，正在革新人们对翻译的既成印象。原文不再是讨论翻译问题的唯一准绳，人们认识到翻译已经把一个文本变成了原文，而并没有影响源语文化中的该文本，因此，原文也并非比译文好，或比译文更权威。原文可由多个来源构成，翻译可重复使用以前的译文。工业产品和本地化手册同步上市，书籍、电影、国际新闻等全球同步出现，欧盟的正式文件有23种不同语言的版本，这些翻译现象甚至使得原文这个概念不复存在。因此，翻译的本质是基于源语文化而在目的语中创作的文本。对实用文献翻译的分析、从职业翻译语境出发进行的翻译研究，必然使翻译的理论与实践建立起更加直接的联系。然而，目前我们对非文学（实用文献）翻译的研究和理论思考却远远不够，人们的翻译观念大多仍然停留在宗教典籍翻译和文学翻译阶段，并且总是试图以这两个阶段的翻译观念来看待甚至解释当今的翻译事实和翻译理论，从而产生了不少困惑乃至抵触，因此，译学观念的现代化势在必行。

西方翻译研究在20世纪下半叶出现了两次"质"的飞跃：一次是把语言学理论引入了翻译研究领域，出现了翻译研究的"语言学转向"，结构主义、交际理论、语言学理论等成为翻译理论的基础；另一次是把翻译研究置于文化语境、历史和传统等更为广阔的领域中展开，出现了翻译研究的"文化转向"，从而使翻译研究发展成为一门独立的学科。20世纪下半叶以来的当代西方翻译理论实现了三个根本性的突破：（1）翻译研究开始从一般层面上的语言间的对等研究深入到了对翻译行为本身的深层探究；（2）翻译研究不再局限于翻译文本本身的研究，而是把目光投射到了译作的生产和消费过程；

（3）翻译研究不再把翻译看成语言转换间的孤立片段，而是把翻译放到一个宏大的文化语境中去审视。不难发现，当代西方翻译所处的文化语境、翻译的内涵以及翻译研究的内容都已经发生了变化。因此可以说，翻译研究的学科化，是翻译从业者职业化、翻译行业产业化、译学观念现代化的必然结果。

第 2 章

翻 译 概 述

翻译是不同国家、不同种族的人们相互沟通的桥梁,是不同思想、文化相互交流,科学、技术相互促进的重要手段,是人类社会发展和进步的需要。

《圣经·旧约》中记载,大洪水之后,上帝和人类以彩虹为记,承诺洪水不会再次泛滥,诺亚的子孙们开始过上稳定的生活,他们在一处大平原定居,因为所有人都讲同一种语言,所以沟通起来非常便捷。为了避免后代们再次遭到洪水的侵害,他们决定建一座城,并在城中修建一座通天的高塔——巴别塔(The Tower of Babel),以相互传递信息。然而,上帝发觉自己的誓言受到了怀疑,于是决定惩罚这些忘记约定的人们,让人们说不同的语言,使人们相互之间不能沟通。因此,建造巴别塔的计划搁置了,人类自此各散东西,逐渐形成不同的民族和国家,有自己不同的语言。《圣经》中巴别塔的典故为世界上存在不同语言和不同种族提供了解释,也很好地诠释了西方人对翻译的巴别塔情节。

第1节 翻译的定义

什么是翻译？在不同的国家、不同的历史时期、不同的学科领域中其定义也不尽相同。《辞海》中把翻译定义为："把一种语言文字的意义用另一种语言文字表达出来。"《牛津英语词典》中翻译的定义是："The action or process of turning from one language into another; also, the product of this; a version in a different language." 英国著名语言学家和翻译理论家卡特·福德（Catford）把翻译定义为："The replacement of textural material in one language (SL) by equivalent textual material in another language (TL)." 其中，SL指的是源语（Source Language），也可译为译出语，TL指的是目标语（Target Language），也可译为译入语（Receptor Language）。

苏联语言学家巴尔胡达罗夫（Barhudarov）在其著作《语言与翻译》一书中指出："Translation is a process in which the parole of one language is transferred into the parole of another with the content i. e. meaning unchanged." 在这个定义中，巴尔胡达罗夫强调了在翻译过程中，相对于语言形式的保留，意义传达的重要性。

在众多的翻译定义中，美国翻译理论家尤金·奈达（Eugene Nida）和英国翻译界元老彼得·纽马克（Peter Newmark）对翻译的定义最为知名，被广泛引用。其中奈达把翻译定义为："Translating consists in reproducing in the receptor language the closest natural equivalent of the source language message, first in terms of meaning and secondly in terms of style." 在这一定义中，我们可以看出，翻译是涉及两种语言（source language 和 receptor language）的转换过程。在这一过程中，译者的目标为在译入语中找到源语"最接近自然等值体"，即找到两种语言中的对等语或对等表达形式。这种对等包括两个方面，即意义的对等和文体的对等。

纽马克对翻译的定义是："Translation is first a science, which entails the knowledge and verification of the facts and the language that describes them here, what is wrong, mistakes of truth, can be identified; secondly, it is a skill, which calls for appropriate language and acceptable usage; thirdly, an art, which distinguishes good from undistinguished writing and is the creative, the intuitive, sometimes the inspired, level of the translation; lastly, a matter of taste, where argument ceases, preferences are expressed, and the variety of meritorious translation is the reflection of individual differences." 从纽马克对翻译的定义中，我们可以看

出，翻译是一门科学。其之所以是一门科学，是因为翻译有许多内在的规律，有许多翻译方法和技巧我们可以运用和遵循，这也使翻译成为一门科学具备可能性。同时，有许多翻译理论家也认为翻译是一门艺术，因为翻译过程是一种再创造过程。郭沫若曾说"翻译是一种创造性的工作，好的翻译等于创作，甚至还可能超过创作。"翻译究竟是一门科学，还是一门艺术，或者二者兼而有之，一直是翻译界争论的焦点。

第 2 节　翻译的类别

根据不同的原则，可以对翻译进行不同的分类。

翻译本质上是一种语言的转换。从翻译涉及的两种语言——译入语和译出语的角度来看，翻译可以分为本族语译为外语和外语译为本族语。例如，我们在进行英汉互译时，包含英语译为汉语和汉语译为英语。国内外的许多专家学者认为，在翻译过程中，人们擅长做的是外语译为本族语，但由于各种语言之间信息译入的不对等，为了文化交流的需要，本族语译为外语也占较大的比例。

从涉及的语言符号来分类，布拉格学派的创始人之一约翰·雅各布逊把符号学引入翻译研究，把翻译分为语内翻译、语际翻译和符际翻译。语内翻译是指在同一语言内部把一些语言符号译为另一些语言符号。例如乔叟的《坎特伯雷故事集》原文为古英语，我们现在看到的多为现代英语翻译。这种从古英语译为现代英语即为一种语内翻译。语际翻译，即不同语言之间的翻译，是最常见的翻译形式，在不同国家、民族之间的政治、经济、文化交往中起着不可或缺的作用。符际翻译是指非语言符号系统和语言符号系统之间的翻译，例如把旗语或摩斯密码翻译为人们能理解的语言符号。

从翻译的手段来分类，翻译可分为口译、笔译和机器翻译。口译和笔译是翻译的两大方向。口译按传送方式可细分为同声传译、交替传译、耳语传译等。机器翻译是利用计算机把一种语言转换成另一种语言的过程。近年来，不少机器翻译软件被广泛运用，辅助传统口笔译，大大提高了翻译效率。

从翻译的体裁来分类，翻译可分为应用文体翻译、科技文体翻译、论述文体翻译、新闻文体翻译、艺术文体翻译等类别，每种体裁的翻译除了具备翻译的共同点外，还有自己的特点，翻译时需要特别注意。

从翻译的处理方式来分类，翻译可分为全译、摘译和编译。全译是指完整地将外文译为目的语。摘译是指挑选能满足某种需要的或受他人指定的或译者本人最感兴趣的部分来加以翻译。编译是指不严格地按照原文翻译，而是选择性地翻译，同时增加译者个人的一些创作。

第3节 翻译标准

翻译标准既是翻译过程中译者所遵循的原则,也是翻译批评家批评译文时需遵循的原则。它是翻译理论的核心问题之一,也是人们研究和探讨得最多的一个话题。在不同的历史时期、不同的学科领域,有对翻译标准的不同理解和表述,国内外译界也在"什么是翻译的标准"这一问题上没有达成共识。总的说来,翻译标准大体可分为以下三种。

3.1 归化与异化

我国翻译历史始于2 000年前东汉时期的佛经翻译,西方翻译历史可以追溯到2 000年前的古罗马时代。在翻译初始之期,就有了直译和意译之争。在此基础上,直译和意译进一步延伸,形成了归化和异化两个概念。归化和异化这对翻译术语是由美国著名翻译理论学家劳伦斯·韦努蒂(Lawrence Venuti)于1995年在《译者的隐身》中提出来的。归化(domestication)是指以目标语读者为核心,采取其所习惯的表达方式来传达原文的内容。这种方法有助于译文读者更好地理解译文,最大限度地淡化原文的陌生感,以达到译入语和译出语之间的对等。美国当代翻译理论家尤金·奈达是归化翻译的代表人物。他所提出的功能对等和动态对等旨在在译入语中找到"最接近自然等值体"。此外,我国三国时期的支谦、东晋时期的鸠摩罗什,西方古罗马时期的西塞罗、贺拉斯等也持这类观点。

异化(foreignization)是指在翻译中尽量保留译出语的语言和文化特点,为译文读者保留异国情调,以促进文化间的交流,丰富译入语的语言形式。在这种翻译原则的指导下,直译、音译等翻译方法得到大量采用,以翻译两种语言、文化中出现的对应空缺之处。持这种原则的翻译家也为数不少,如我国西晋时期的佛经翻译家竺法护、美国著名作家赛珍珠等。

归化和异化表面看起来是两种完全对立的翻译策略和原则。但是在实际翻译过程中,我们既不能完全归化,也不能完全异化。译者应找到二者的融合点,使译文既能保持原文的特点,又符合译入语的表达习惯。

3.2 忠实与通顺

英语专业八级翻译的测试要求中指出译文必须忠实原意,语言通顺、流畅。可见,忠实与通顺是翻译中的基本原则。我国唐代翻译巨匠玄奘提出的翻译时"既须求真,又须喻俗",英国18世纪最著名的翻译理论家亚历山大·

泰特勒（Tytler）在其《论翻译的原则》一书中提出的翻译三原则（译文应完全复写出原作的思想；译文的风格和笔调应与原文的性质相同；译文应和原作同样流畅）都属于这类翻译原则。

在这一原则中，最为知名的应属我国清末时期的著名学者严复于1898年在《天演论》（译例言）中提出的"信、达、雅"三字标准。其后，鲁迅提出"凡是翻译，必须兼顾两方面：一当然力求其易解；二则保存着原作的丰姿"；林语堂则提出"忠实标准、通顺标准、美的标准"；刘重德提出"信、达、切"三字标准。这类翻译标准在表达上用词可能不尽相同，但都围绕着"忠实"与"通顺"这两方面。

我国当代翻译理论家张培基在其《英汉翻译教程》中对"忠实""通顺"做了进一步的解释。这类翻译原则的共同特点是：翻译既要"忠实"，又要"通顺"，即译文必须既要考虑到原作者，又要考虑到译文的读者。用张培基等人的话说就是："所谓忠实，首先指忠实于原作的内容。译者必须把原作的内容完整而准确地表达出来，不得有任何篡改、歪曲、遗漏阉割或任意增删的现象。""所谓通顺，即指译文语言必须通顺易懂，符合规范。译文必须是明白晓畅的现代语言，没有逐词死译、硬译的现象，没有语言晦涩难懂、佶屈聱牙的现象，没有文理不通、结构混乱、逻辑不清的现象。"

从翻译实践来看，这类翻译原则是可行的，但缺点是过于笼统和抽象，如何真正做到既"忠实"又"通顺"是很难把握的。

3.3 美学翻译原则

以美学为取向的翻译原则主要为文学翻译家所提倡。例如：美国的著名意象派诗人庞德（Pound）极为重视诗歌翻译中意象的传达。他认为译诗对原诗意象的传达和再创造是诗歌翻译的核心问题。苏联著名翻译家加切奇拉泽认为对文学译作的评判应以艺术效果的转换而不是字、词、句或篇章等语言层次的转换是否等值为标准。同样，我国现当代翻译家傅雷从文艺学与美学角度提出翻译的最高艺术境界是"神似"，著名学者钱钟书提出文学翻译的最高标准是"化境"，许渊冲先生提出"意美、音美、形美"之"三美论"。以美学为取向的翻译原则多适合于文学翻译；以此指导翻译实践的确产生了不少精彩的文学译作。但是，该原则对于不少人来说显得过于高深和抽象，同时也不太适合用来指导非文学作品的翻译实践。

第 4 节　翻译的过程

西方翻译界常将翻译前的各种准备工作,甚至包括与出版商打交道,视为翻译过程的组成部分。例如,美国翻译理论家安德烈·勒菲弗尔(Andre Lefevere)在其翻译改写理论中就提出了"意识形态、诗学、赞助人"三大要素。我们这里所谈的翻译过程主要指翻译真正进行的过程,包括理解、表达和校核这三个阶段。

在理解阶段,译者首先需理解原文作者的写作风格和特点以及原文创作的时代背景、作品的内容和作品主题。之后需要对原作文本进行解读,包括语句的语法分析、词的语义分析、文章的语体分析和语篇分析等方面。对原文全面的理解是译好原文的基础。

表达阶段是译文能否成功的最关键阶段,是对译文理解的外化表现。在这一过程中,译者既要再现原文的内容和风格,又要保持译文符合译入语的表达习惯。灵活运用增减、分合、语序调整等各种翻译方法和技巧,在遣词组句、组句成篇上下功夫。

校核是翻译中对译文进行全面检查的阶段,是改进译文的大好时机。在出版社和翻译公司,一般对译文都会进行数次校对。对一般翻译者来说,建议对译文至少进行两次校对。第一次校对译文是否有漏译、误译之处,即检查译文是否忠实于原文;第二次校对译文是否符合译入语的表达习惯,即检查译文是否通顺。

第 5 节　译者的素质

译者，作为翻译活动的主体，在翻译过程中起着决定性的作用。好的译者能在原作和读者之间架起良好的沟通桥梁。莫言获得诺贝尔文学奖，其作品译者葛浩文起了重要的作用。要成为一名好的译者，其各方面的素质必须过硬。

第一，做好翻译工作要具备良好的政治素质，要了解党和国家的方针政策，工作态度认真严谨。第二，译者需要具有良好的双语能力，具有母语和目的语扎实的语言基本功，能灵活地穿梭于双语中，熟练地进行语言转换输出。第三，译者需要具有丰富的文化知识和专业知识，熟悉母语和目的语国家国情历史、社会文化或是政治经济、科学技术、商贸金融等方面的专业知识，努力做一个"杂家"。第四，译者要熟悉翻译理论和常用翻译方法和技巧，能灵活运用各种翻译技巧。翻译理论和翻译技巧都是翻译学家在多年的翻译实践中总结、积累的，对个人翻译实践有很好的指导作用。第五，译者要熟悉各种翻译工具书，在翻译工程中遇到难题时要多查多问，知道怎样去查找正确的答案。此外，译者还要熟悉各种翻译软件，利用现在科学技术，提高翻译效率。

第3章

英汉语言对比

语言是人类所特有的、用任意符号来表达感情、愿望和交流思想的基本手段。从语言学的层面上看，英语和汉语分属于不同的语言系统。英语属于印欧语系（Indo-European language family）。这一语系中的各语言原来都是屈折语（fusional language/inflectional language）。其特点为：名词和大部分形容词有格、性和数的变化；词缀和词干元音音变表达语法意义；动词有时态、语态和语体的变化，主语和动词在变化中互相呼应；词有重音。随着语言的发展变化，以英语为代表的一些印欧语系语言形态已经简化，开始向分析语（analytical language）转化。汉语属于汉藏语系（Sino-Tibetan language family）。这一语系的特点是有很多孤立语（isolating language）、分析语；有声调变化；单音节词根在语言中占大多数；有量词；以虚词和语序作为表达语法意义的主要手段。

语言是人类表达思维的工具，是各民族文化的载体。由于生态、历史、宗教、民情、习俗等方面的不同，英语民族与汉语民族思维方式也就不尽相同，因而他们的作为思维工具和文化载体的语言也存在不少差异。

第 1 节　英汉语言宏观对比

英汉两种语言文化环境不同，其宏观表达方面必然存在着特定的差异。在思维方式和文化上，中国人强调伦理，西方人注重认知；中国人习惯主体思维，英美人习惯客体思维；中国人注重整体，西方人强调个体；中国人侧重直觉，西方人侧重实证；中国人倾向于形象思维，英美人倾向于逻辑思维。基于上述中西方在文化和思维方式上的差异，以连淑能先生为代表的一些语言学家，把英、汉两种语言在语言结构上的宏观差异归纳为十点：综合型与分析型、刚性与柔性、形合与意合、繁复与简短、物称与人称、被动与主动、静态与动态、抽象与具体、间接与直接、替代与重复。了解这些差异，可以为英汉翻译打下基础，帮助我们更好地进行英汉翻译。在英汉语言结构的十大差异中，形合与意合、物称与人称、静态与动态、抽象与具体、替代与重复这五点尤为突出，下面将重点分析。

1.1　形合与意合

西方人逻辑理性思维发达，从亚里士多德的形式逻辑到 16—18 世纪欧洲的理性主义，一直强调科学实验，注重形式论证。西方民族这种重分析、重形式、重（逻辑）理性的思维习惯在语言表达上体现为非常重视可分析性和形式逻辑。而汉语言民族直觉思维发达，具有悠久的整体论辩证思维哲学传统，因而在语言表达上具有较强的情感性和直观性。汉语言民族这种着眼整体、重悟性的思维模式，在语言构建上表现为注重构成部分内在的意义关系。我国现代语言学先驱王力教授在《中国语法理论》一书中指出，形合和意合是语言的两种基本组织手段。"形合"（hypotaxis），又称"显性"（explicitness/overtness），指借助语言形式，主要包括词汇手段和形态手段，实现词语或句子的连接。"意合"（parataxis），也称"隐性"（implicitness/covertness）或"零形式连接"，指不借助于语言形式，而借助于词语或句子所含意义的逻辑联系来实现语篇内部的连接。形合性语言注重语言形式上的对应（cohesion），意合性语言注重行文意义上的连贯（coherence）。因而汉语句子的特点是"以意统形"，强调逻辑关系和意义关联而不在意词语之间和句子之间的形式衔接，整体看是意合句。英语句子的特点是强调形式和功能，句子之间的各个成分要通过相应的连接词和关联词语表示其中的关系，整体上看是形合句。例如：

1. <u>If</u> winter comes, can spring be far behind?

2. That is my sister who is sitting by the window.

3. 即使你去了那里，也不会有什么结果。

在上面的三个例子中，"if"，"who"和"即使……也"这些关联词语清晰地表示了句子之间的逻辑关系。我们再来看另外三个例子：

4. 知己知彼，百战不殆。

5. 他来了，我走。

6. The earlier, the better.

这三个例子中，没有第一组的那些关联词语，句子之间的关系是由内在逻辑关系和句子前后顺序决定的。

通过上面六个例子，我们可以看出英语句子整体上看是形合句，但也有一些句子，特别是习语、谚语等，属于意合句。汉语句子整体上看是意合句，但在一些情况下，也可以用连词、介词、虚词等连接，以更清楚地表达出句子成分之间的关系。

英语作为形合性的语言，其词连接成句，短语连接成句，分句连接成句，往往都离不开连词（如 and, but, or 等并列连词；if, because, since, unless 等从属连词）、关系词（如关系代词 that, which, who 等；关系副词 when, where, why 等）、介词（如 on, in, of 等）。在英译汉中，这些关联词语往往可以省略，以使汉语译文更加简洁，但在省译这些关联词语的过程中，不少情况下需要进行语序调整，以符合汉语句子意合特点：突出表现时间、逻辑的先后顺序，按时间先后顺序和事理推移的方法，一件事一件事交代清楚，一层一层铺开，分句以并列为主，呈竹节式排列。例如：

7. If you confer a benefit, never remember it; if you receive one, remember it always.

原译：如果你给他人好处，不要记住它；如果你得到好处，则永远记住它。

改译：施恩勿记，受恩勿忘。

在上面的例子中，原译保留了原文的两个"if"，虽然也译出了原文的意思，但不如省译连接词后的改译更加简单明晰、符合汉语表达习惯。再如：

8. As I lie awake in bed, listening to the sound of those razor-sharp drops pounding on the pavement, my mind goes reeling down dark corridors teeming with agonizing flashbacks, and a chill from within fills me with dread.

9. All was cleared up some time later when news came from a distant place that an earthquake was felt the very day the little copper ball fell.

需要注意的是，有时，英语句子中连接词起强调作用或省译连接词后句子关系表达不清晰。在这种情况下，英译汉时需保留连接词。例如：

10. It is due to the development of integrate circuits that there is possibility to make electronic devices smaller and smaller.

正是由于集成电路的研制成功，才有可能把电子器件做得越来越小。

上句是由"it is... that..."引导的强调句型，在译为汉语时，保留了"正是……才……"，以更清楚地表达句子之间的关系。再如：

11. Despite the privation, and the mounting toll of dead and wounded, however, morale remained intact, and people still smiled in the street.

此外，还有一些特殊情况，如当原文主语、宾语较长需要分译时，或"for, with"等介词不能清晰表达原文句子内部关系时，不但不可省略连接词，还要添加连接词。例如：

12. The effectiveness of the electronic computer lies in its great speed and accuracy in calculation.

电子计算机之所以效率高，是因为其运算速度快、计算精确。

上句中主语和宾语较长，并且都表达了独立、完整的意思，我们在译为汉语时进行了分译，并增加了"因为"这一连接词来表明分句之间的关系。再如：

13. A symbol of abundance to the rest of the world, the Amazon is experiencing a crisis of overfishing.

14. With all its disadvantages, this design is considered to be one of the best.

15. New Zealand music has been influenced by blues, jazz, country, rock and roll and hip hop, with many of these genres given a unique New Zealand interpretation.

当然，英语中还有不少习语、谚语，其语法结构不像正常语句那样严谨，句子成分之间没有关联词语连接，表现出意合句的特点。在这种情况下，往往可直接译为汉语意合句。例如：

16. Out of sight, out of mind.

眼不见，心不想。

综上所述，英译汉时连接词的增减需要与具体的语境联系起来。在确立衔接和连贯关系时，需考虑源语读者和目标语读者的理解能力和接受度。

1.2 物称与人称

中国的文化和思维通常以人为出发点，从人的角度去观察和描述外部世界，因而汉语常用人或有生命的词作主语或在实在没有主语的情况下，使用无主语句的表达形式。而西方哲学讲究主客二分，注重客体以及对客观世界的认识和研究，语言表达上常用无生命的词作主语，也称为无灵主语，以客观方式陈述客观事实。据统计，英语句子有50%的句子主语是抽象名词、无生命的事物名称、非人称代词"it"或"there（be）"结构。

英语用物称或非生命的名词作主语的句子，结构严密紧凑，言简意赅。许多句子从语法分析看属于简单句，但它们表达出了复合句或并列句的语义和逻辑关系。英译汉时常常要转换非人称主语为人称主语，或译为汉语中的泛指主语句或无主语句，并采用转译、分译、增词等翻译方法和技巧。例如：

1. The invitation to me from the British Broadcasting Corporation was to present the development of science in a series of television programmes.

英国广播公司邀请我通过一套电视节目来表现科学的发展过程。

在上面的例子中，英语原文中的主语为"invitation"，在汉译时，我们选择"英国广播公司"作主语更符合汉语表达习惯。再如：

2. But recently, fear has settled in.

3. The mastery of a language requires painstaking efforts.

4. So the thought crossed his mind: maybe it did not have to end. Maybe he would take a break from college and keep working.

5. The political upheaval in Libya and elsewhere in North Africa has opened the way for thousands of new migrants to make their way to Europe across the Mediterranean.

1.3 静态与动态

英语里，动词经常被弱化或虚化。英语最常用的动词是动作意味最弱的动词,即"to be"的各种形式;此外,"have, become, grow, feel, go, come, get, do"等也是英语常用的弱势动词。英语还常常把动词转化或派生成名词,置于弱势动词之后作其宾语,如"have a rest, take a walk, make a plan"等,或采用非谓语动词的形式(如名词、介词、形容词、副词等)表达动词的意义,整体表达呈静态。而汉语句子中动词使用较多,在表示动作时多用动词。另外,汉语动词及动词词组,包括连动式词组、兼语式词组,无须改变形式就可以充当句子的各种成分,一句话中往往有多个动词,因而汉语是一种动态性语言。基于英、汉两种语言的上述差异,在英译汉时,往往需要进行词类的转换,把英语名词、介词、形容词、副词等转译为汉语动词。例如:

1. Harvard, despite its own estimate of itself, was ultimately an academic heaven where an error of interpretation could result only in loss of face, not in extinction.

哈佛大学,不管它如何自命高明,终究还是个学府胜地,在那里把问题看错了,无非丢脸而已,总不至于完蛋。

在上句中"estimate, interpretation, loss, extinction"四个名词都是动词转化或派生的词,在汉译时都译为了动词,以符合汉语的表达习惯。再如:

2. The doctor's extremely quick arrival and uncommonly careful examination of the patient brought about his very speedy recovery.

3. He has someone behind him.

4. I'm afraid Mr. Brown is out, but he'll be in soon.

1.4 抽象与具体

西方哲学主张以逻辑和理性探索自然规律,透过事物的现象把握事物的本质,这种思维具有较强的抽象性。而中国传统思维习惯将特定的思想寄寓于具体的物象之中,用形象的方式来表达抽象的事物。受中西方思维不同方式的影响,英语属于表音文字,通过26个字母的排列组合表达意思,而汉语的发展则基于象形文字,以象形、会意、指事、形声等方法使汉字达到音、形、义的统一。在表达同一概念时,英语和汉语存在着对立的倾向。一般认为,英语倾向于使用抽象的表达方式而汉语则倾向于使用具体的表达方式,从而在表达法上英语表现出抽象、汉语表现出具体的倾向。例如在汉语中我们说"蒙在鼓里",而英语中对应的表达为"be kept in dark";汉语中的"丢盔卸甲",翻译为英语是"throw away everything","盔"和"甲"都不用翻译出来。因而在英译汉时,一般可对一些抽象的表达进行具体化的引申,例如:

1. Wisdom prepares for the worst, but folly leaves the worst for the day it comes.

聪明人未雨绸缪,愚蠢者临渴掘井。

在上面的翻译中,英文的抽象表达都在译为汉语时进行了具体化处理。再如:

2. He had surfaced with less visibility in the policy decisions.

3. There is more in their life than political and social and economic problems. It is more than transient everydayness.

1.5 替代与重复

英语重替代,除了修辞需要外,很少在句子中重复相同的词或词组,而是用变换或替代相同词语等方法来回避过多的重复。汉语表达讲究匀称,用词倾向于重复,自古以来,就有一种追求均衡、讲究对称的心理。在汉语里,经常出现音、义、词、语、句的重叠反复、成双成对、对立并联和对偶排比。可以说,汉语不怕重复,通过重复往往能使表达清晰、句子或词组对称、读起来朗朗上口。例如:

1. Translation from English into Chinese is not so easy as that from English into French.

英译汉不如英译法容易。

在上面的例子中,英文用"that"替代了"translation",而汉译时对"译"进行了重复。再如:

2. There are rising inequalities within and among countries.

3. He hated failure; he had conquered it all his life, risen above it and despised it in others.

第2节 英汉语言微观对比

英语和汉语除了语言结构方面的主要异同,在词汇方面和语法方面还存在不少微观差异。词汇方面的差异主要体现在词义和词的搭配能力上,语法方面的差异主要体现在词序、词类方面。

2.1 词汇对比

词是具备形、音、义,可独立使用的语言中的最小单位。对译者来说,对词义的理解是翻译的基础,确切理解每句中重点单词的意义,是顺利翻译全文的前提和关键。

2.1.1 英汉语言在词义上的对等关系

美国著名翻译理论家尤金·奈达给翻译的定义是:Translating consists in reproducing in the receptor language the closest natural equivalent of the source language message, first in terms of meaning and secondly in terms of style. 在这个定义中,在目标语中找出原语的对等词是翻译的根本。

英语和汉语词语的对等情况比较复杂。总的来说,可以分为以下五种情况。

2.1.1.1 完全对等

尽管不同的语言之间存在很大的差异,但是它们能够就很多的事情达成共识。一种语言中有些词所表达的意思,在另一种语言中可找到完全对应的词来表达,这种在词义上的对等称为完全对等。在词义完全对等的情况下,可以把原文的信息直接翻译到目标语言中。这是最简单、最高效的翻译方法。例如,英语中的"Bluetooth"译为汉语的"蓝牙技术","Talk show"译为汉语的"脱口秀"等。这种完全对等主要适用于一些专有名词、科技术语和日常用语方面的翻译,并且,随着现代科学技术的发展,国与国之间的交流越来越便捷,许多英语中的新词新语通过直译或音译翻译过来后,也形成了与汉语译文的完全对等。再如:

1. bungie jumping

tycoon

job hop

laser

使用完全对等这种方法的前提条件是原文的语言和目标语对同一概念有相同的理解和相同的描述。也就是说,这种词义上的完全对等既包括指

称意义上的对等,也包括蕴含意义上的对等。在寻找完全对等的对应词语时,容易找到假的对应词,我们在翻译时需特别注意。例如:

2. black tea 红茶

英语中的"black tea"不能根据"black"和"tea"两个词的指称意义直接对应成汉语的表达,以免找到错误的对应词。再如:

3. press conference

4. in the same boat

2.1.1.2　一词多义

我们在英译汉时,经常会有英语和汉语词义大小不相等的感觉。原因在于,我们在学习一个单词时,往往只学习了它的基本含义或某一方面的含义,而在英语中一词多义的现象十分普遍。随便打开一本英语词典,我们可以看到大多数的英语单词,即便是最简单的"a, an, the"等单词,也都会有不低于十条的词义,而汉语的词义相对来说比较固定,因而在翻译时我们往往需要根据搭配和上下文来判断某个英语单词的词义。

我们前面提到过,中国人注重伦理,西方人注重认知,这一点可以从亲属称谓上清晰体现。以英语中的"cousin"一词为例,它可以指男性或女性、比说话人年长或年幼、父系或母系的同辈亲属。在汉语中,可对应为堂兄、堂弟、堂姐、堂妹、表哥、表弟、表姐、表妹等一系列亲属关系。而英文中只有"cousin"一词,或在其后加上"Tom, Daisy"等名字来加以区别。我们在英译汉时,需要根据上下文来翻译词语的具体词义,例如:

1. In his classic novel, *The Pioneers*, James Fenimore Cooper has his hero, a land developer, take his cousin on a tour of the city he is building. He describes the broad streets, rows of houses, a teeming metropolis. But his cousin looks around bewildered. All she sees is a forest.

詹姆士·菲尼摩尔·库珀在其经典小说《开拓者》中,让主人公,即一个土地开发商,带他的表妹游览正在由他承建的一座城市。他描述了宽阔的街道、林立的房屋、热闹的都市。但是,他的表妹环顾四周,大感不解。她所看到的是一片森林。

通过上下文,我们发现,这里"cousin"指的是女性,因而可以翻译为堂姐、堂妹,或表姐、表妹。又如:

2. President

再如关于"run"一词,我们所熟悉的基本含义是"跑",但在下面的例子中，它显然不是"跑"之意。

3. Now in addition to running her restaurant, she has one of the most popular stalls there.

请判断"charge"一词在下面句子中的含义。

4. Your future phone may never need to be charged.

5. All goods are delivered free of charge.

6. The opposition was quick to reply to the charge.

2.1.1.3 多词同义

多词同义这种对等形式在英汉词汇对等中也十分普遍。很多时候，对于英语中的同一个义项，在汉译时需要采用不同的译法。这些译法往往基本意思相同，但所表达的语气强弱、感情色彩、适应的人物身份、正式程度等不同。因而，在翻译这类词时，我们要注意推敲译文中词的大小、轻重、语体风格，选择恰当的词与之对应。例如，"potato"一词可以译为马铃薯或土豆，但前者明显比后者正式，多用于书面语，如介绍马铃薯这种作物的科普文章；后者则更多地应用于日常用语中。此外，在一些方言中，potato 还可译为"洋芋、地豆、山药蛋"等。

请翻译"wife, semiannual"两词，并从词义大小、轻重、语体风格等方面比较不同译文。

1. wife

2. semiannual

我们熟悉的 celebration 一词一般为庆祝之意，请看下面例子中译文在词义选择时是否做到了感情色彩恰当。

3. People attended the city's annual "Earth Day" celebration.

原译：许多人参加了市里举办的"地球日"庆祝活动。

改译：

2.1.1.4 词义相异

词义相异主要指中西方一些文化负载词在语义上的差异，一般包括两种情况：第一种情况是词的指称意义相符，但词的社会意义、情感意义、联想意义、引申意义、比喻意义等蕴含意义不同。以"西风"为例，汉语中的"西风"和英语中的"west wind"指称意义相同，但在汉语中，西风盛行于冬季，寒冷而干燥，所以就有"古道西风瘦马，夕阳西下，断肠人在天涯"的凄凉描述。而英国位于欧亚大陆的西北，西风的蕴含意义与中国完全相反，所以英国作家梅斯菲尔德赞美西风："It's a warm wind, the west wind, full of birds cries…"，而著名诗人雪莱则在《西风颂》中把西风比作革命的力量。

第二种情况是指称意义与蕴含意义都相异。例如，汉语"龙"的指称意义是一种神异动物，具有九种动物合而为一之九不像之形象，为兼备各种动物之所长的异类，在中国文化中常与帝王联系在一起。而英文中龙的对应词"Dragon"的指称意义是"an imaginary animal with wings and claws, able to breathe out fire"。英语中第一首叙事长诗《贝奥武夫》（*Beowulf*）中就出现了"Fire dragon"（火龙）的恶魔形象。可见，在西方文化中，"dragon"一词的蕴含意义常指凶残的有翼巨兽、恶魔、悍妇等，与汉语中"龙"的蕴含意义完全相反。北京奥运会之前，对如何翻译"龙"曾发生过广泛的争论，有人提议把"龙"译为"long"，但目前通用的翻译还是"dragon"，例如BBC在2016年推出的三集纪录片《中国新年》中提到龙年，舞龙等都用的"dragon"一词。

对于词义相异现象，一般在翻译时，我们常使用直译，把源语中的文化内涵在译文中加以体现，以期能在读者脑海中引起相似的联想和理解，进而认识民族特性和其独有的文化内涵，从而通过在译语中尽量再现源语的文化信息，真正达到文化传播交流的目的。

2.1.1.5 词义空缺

每个国家的文化都有其鲜明的民族特色，并通过语言体现出来，词义空缺就是一个典型的例子。因此在翻译中，经常会出现在两种语言互译时找不到对应词的情况。在这种情况下，翻译时需要用音译、意译、释义等方式翻译其义。以"shuttle bus"为例，"shuttle"的本义是"梭子"，这里指许多机场采用的一种专用的客车，往返于主楼与各个候机楼之间运载旅客。根据"shuttle bus"的具体功能，汉译时可用释义法翻译为"摆渡车"。"pumpkin-eater"也是一个很好的例子。它源于一个童谣："Peter, Peter, pumpkin eater, had a wife and couldn't keep her."因而，根据这一出处，可以把"pumpkin-eater"译成"养不活老婆的人"。又如：

1. clock-watcher

2. redshirt

3. swan song

2.1.2 词的搭配能力

英、汉两种语言在搭配能力上有不小的差异。总的来说，英语的搭配能力较强，越是常用的词，与其他词搭配而成固定表达的概率就越高。而相对而言，汉语的搭配能力较弱。因而在英译汉时，对同一单词，我们要根据不同的搭配确定词义。例如：

1. fast　　the fast growth：迅速发展
　　　　　fast color：不褪掉的颜色
　　　　　a fast oven：烤箱
　　　　　fast asleep：熟睡的
　　　　　stick fast in the mud：牢牢地陷在泥巴里

在上面的一组例子中，"fast"一词在不同的搭配中被译为了不同的意思。再来看看我们非常熟悉的"open"一词在不同搭配中的含义。

2. open　　an open book：
　　　　　an open question：
　　　　　open wires：
　　　　　open speech：

翻译下面的句子，注意画线词在不同搭配中的不同词义。

3. A lack of electricity has <u>stymied</u> economic development, literacy rates and health in these rural regions.

4. But his attack was always <u>repulsed</u> by a kick or a blow from a stick.

2.2 语法对比

英、汉两种语言在语法方面既有相似之处又有不同之处。掌握英汉两种语言的语法差异是帮助我们解决英汉翻译中存在的障碍的有效途径。英、汉两种语言在语法方面的差异主要体现在句内语序和句间语序两个方面。

2.2.1 句内语序

在句内语序方面，英语和汉语这两种语言句子的主要成分都包括主语、谓语、宾语或表语。它们的语序在英语和汉语中基本一致。但是状语和定语的位置比较复杂，在两种语言中有异有同。

汉语的基本句子模式是：

主语+状语+谓语+宾语（定语通常位于主语和宾语之前）

英语的基本句子模式是：

主语+谓语+宾语+状语（较长的定语必须放在所修饰词的后面）

由上述英、汉两种语言在句子基本模式上的比较可见，翻译时应把重点放在定语和状语的位置上。

2.2.1.1　定语的位置

英语中单个单词作定语通常放在所修饰词的前面，这一点和汉语一致。但当多个单词并列作定语时，译为汉语时需调整语序，因为英语把对中心词最本质的修饰词放在离中心词最近的位置，而汉语则恰恰相反，如：

1. local culture

2. a famous American university

英语中单个单词作定语时也有后置情况，如形容词修饰不定代词"any，something，nothing"等，或表语形容词作定语、单个副词作定语等情况。在这些情况下，译为汉语时，定语需提前，译为汉语中的前置定语。例如：

3. anything new

4. the guests present

5. the passage above

英语中短语作定语通常放在所修饰词的后面，译为汉语时需要前置。例如：

6. education on first aid knowledge

7. an apartment with two bedrooms and one living room

8. Any event attended by the actor received widespread media coverage.

此外，如果原文中名词前的定语过多，汉译时不宜完全前置，以避免表达过于冗长、啰唆，例如：

7. a little, yellow, ragged, lame, unshaven beggar

2.2.1.2 状语的位置

英语中单个单词作状语通常放在它所修饰词的前面，这一点与汉语相同。短语作状语时，英语中可前置可后置，而译成汉语时，大多数放在所修饰动词之前，而在少数情况下也可视表达习惯放在后面。当一个句子中既有时间状语又有地点状语和方式状语时，英文中的习惯顺序是先方式状语，后地点状语，最后是时间状语，汉语则恰恰相反。此外，在时间状语和地点状语内部，汉语的时间顺序由大到小，即先说"年"，再说"月"，最后才说"日"、"时"等；地点上遵循国、省、市、县、乡、村等的顺序，而英语一般为由小及大的顺序。例如：

1. IT industry has been developing rapidly in these years.

近年来 IT 业一直在迅速发展。

在上面的例子中，英文中的状语"rapidly"和"in these years"位于句尾，译为汉语时，根据汉语表达习惯，分别调至了句首和主谓之间。再如：

2. My uncle passed away in hospital at 2：30 a. m. on September 12, 1999.

3. They discussed the plan animatedly in the classroom yesterday afternoon.

2.2.2 句间语序

在主从复合句中，英语和汉语的句间语序不同。西方人习惯于开门见山，先说明要点，或表明态度和观点，然后再叙事，阐述事情的原因或发生的条件。中国人习惯从侧面说出，先阐述外围的环境，最后点出话语的信息中心；通常表现为先摆明事情的来龙去脉，把事情或情况说清楚，再表明自己的态度和观点，给出一个简单的表态或评论。例如：

1. Their booking could be cancelled at the last minute if the weather is bad.

但如果天气不好，他们的预订可能会在最后一刻被取消。

在上面的例子中，英文"if"所引导的状语从句位于句尾，而在汉语译文中根据逻辑顺序应该前置。再如：

2. It makes no sense to throw perfectly good products away, just because they are the "wrong" shape.

了解和掌握英、汉两种语言的对比十分重要。任何翻译方法、技巧、理论都是建立在两种语言的对比分析上的。另外，译者只有掌握两种语言的不同，才能在两种语言的转换上游刃有余，从而翻译出高水平的译文。

练习

一、翻译下列句子,注意英汉语言的宏观差异。

1. A fall into the pit, a gain in your wit.

2. Even if you go there, there wouldn't be any result.

3. This failure to recognize and analyze the interrelationship of linguistic and non-linguistic problems produces two major signs of ineffectiveness.

4. His greatness is attributed by his biographers and critics not alone to his profound medical knowledge and insight but to his broad general education, for he was a very cultured man.

5. That Christmas, which my father had planned so carefully, was it the best or the worst I ever knew? He often asked me that; I never could answer as a boy. I think now that it was both. It covered the whole distance from broken-hearted misery to bursting happiness—too fast. A grown-up could hardly have stood it.

6. The truth finally dawned on him.

7. The thick carpet killed the sound of his footsteps.

8. Dusk found her crying in the park.

9. A little flattery will fetch him.

10. His being neglected by the host added to his uneasiness.

11. The early 1600s saw the beginning of a great tide of emigration from Europe to North America.

12. Friday started with a morning visit to the modern campus of the 22,000-student University of Michigan in nearby Ann Arbor, where the Chinese table tennis

team joined students in the cafeteria line for lunch and later played an exhibition match.

13. A lack of information and formal educational training had left many persons without any generalized standards of judgment applicable to this novel situation.

14. Is this train for Chicago?

15. Down with the old and up with the new.

16. I am afraid of your misunderstanding me.

17. He was a clever man; a pleasant companion; a careless student; with a great propensity for running into debt, and a partiality for the tavern.

18. So instead of descending the road to that station we crossed it by the traffic lights and went through the narrow lanes to my apartment building.

19. With this medical box at the ready, you'll be able to deal with the slight illness by yourself.

20. Work with, and not against, nature.

二、翻译下列句子或短语，注意英、汉语言的微观差异。

1. ecocide

2. coffee mate

3. Pyswar

4. satellite town

5. Naderism

6. (1) oral message

   (2) congratulatory message

   (3) message centre

   (4) send a person on a message

7. the ancient Chinese alchemists

8. (1) Our relation with Germany was excellent.

   (2) Here I discontinue my relation of the American Revolution.

9. The technology could save time and money in the production process and will allow for greater customization.

10. Needing some light to see by, the burglar crossed the room with a light step to light the light with the light green shade.

11. (1) He was wearing a toothpick in his mouth at the wheel.

    (2) This was a little man, old, fat and bald, who at first had tried his hardest to wear a severe expression.

    (3) She wears the slimness of her mother.

    (4) She really wears her years well.

    (5) Most of the people you profiled are really entrepreneurs, a title to wear proudly.

12. For further detail, contact: International Language Center, 86 York, London.

13. The meeting is to be held in Room 301 at 9 tomorrow morning.

14. The communication satellite can provide effectively voice and data signals to any place and at any time.

15. These days it is hard to find a big city that doesn't make grandiose claims to encourage cycling, and harder still to find one that fulfills them.

三、段落翻译

Ancestral Wisdom of the Hand

Today the ancient, ancestral wisdom of the hand has been largely replaced by the simple movements of the machine operator. Our glass and china, furniture, books, and textiles are almost entirely products of the machine. That machine-made goods can be well designed and good-looking no one denies; nevertheless, there are many who believe that if the old skills of the hand-worker were to die out altogether, it would be a disaster.

Their arguments are, roughly, three. First, that the machine is by its nature a mass producer, and that objects made in ones and twos can be made better, even cheaper, by an individual craftsman than by a machine; secondly that the human hand with relatively simple tools can produce objects of a quality permanently beyond the reach of the machine; thirdly, that it is not good for mankind if people lose the ability to create with their hands.

第 4 章

直译与意译

　　直译与意译是翻译过程中最常见的问题，也是两种最基本的翻译方法。"直译""意译"这两个名词虽然在 20 世纪二三十年代才出现，但"直译""意译"之争自翻译开始之时起就已存在。我国的翻译事业始于佛经翻译。我国译经史上始终存在着"质""文"两派。其中，"质"的意思是紧扣原文的表达形式，不进行任何增减，尽量保留原文的语言特点，甚至包括其中不符合汉语表达方式和写作特点的成分；"文"则与"质"相反，要求修饰译文，使之通达，即尽量使译文接近汉语的语言习惯。东晋、前秦时期的佛经翻译家释道安主张直译，唯恐翻译失真；后秦时期翻译名家鸠摩罗什则倾向于意译，常常在翻译中对原文加以改动以适应汉语文体。

　　直译指译者在翻译过程中尽量保持源语文本的基本形式，包括句子结构、词语意思、修辞方法等，是一种既保持原文内容又保持原文形式的翻译方法。意译指译者在翻译中优先照顾源语文本的内容而忽略其形式。这种翻译方法可抛开原文的用词、句法结构、修辞方法，不拘泥于原文的形式，而把重点放在原文意思的传递和表达上。关于如何选择直译与意译，许渊冲先生在《翻译中的几对矛盾》一文中指出："句子的大部分都无所谓直译或意译；译文和原文相同的形式能表达和原文相同的内容时，可以直译；原文的表达形式比译文精确有力时，可以直译，但要符合'忠实'、'通顺'的标准；译文和原文相同的形式不能表达和原文相同的内容时，一般意译；译文的表达形式比原文精确有力时，可以意译。"

第 1 节 直 译 法

对于直译与意译的选择,陆殿扬先生曾提出一条原则:Translate literally, if possible, or appeal to free translation。据统计,大约 70% 的翻译都采用直译法。翻译时,直译优先主要有两方面的原因。首先,在原文中的表达对译文读者来说可理解、可接受的情况下,直译省时省力,是最直接、最高效的翻译方法。例如,"American dream" 直译为 "美国梦","gentlemen's agreement" 直译为 "君子协定"。再如:

1. A "back-to-the-land" movement in the U.S. reversed the decline of small farms in New England and Alaska in the decade from 1970 to 1980.

美国的 "返回田地" 运动扭转了 1970—1980 年这十年间新英格兰和阿拉斯加小农场衰败的局面。

上面的例子中,"back-to-the-land" 直译为了汉语中的 "返回田地",汉语读者完全可理解、可接受。又如:

2. But as the scale grows and the demand for biofuel crops seems to be infinite, we're seeing some negative effects and we need to hold up a yellow light.

3. I hope to avoid straying on the one hand into the sands of foreign policy, and on the other into the marshes of international law.

4. It is now wait-and-see if, say, 10 years down the road, more would choose alternative careers. Hopefully, by then no one would think sportsmen or musicians as making too big a sacrifice in chasing their dreams.

5. Many Chinese companies regard Britain's flexible and open economy as an ideal launching pad into European market.

直译优先的另一个原因是直译保存了原文中包括修辞手法在内的形式,因而能达到与原文近似的语言效果,同时有利于目的语读者了解源语文化信息。例如,"chain reaction" 我们直译为 "连锁反应","Pandora's box" 可直译为 "潘多拉的盒子"。再如:

6. Silicon Valley is a magnet to which numerous talented engineers, scientists and entrepreneurs from overseas flock in search of fame and fast money.

硅谷犹如一块磁铁，吸引着无数才智卓越的工程师、科学家和企业家从世界各地纷至沓来，以求成名并快速积累财富。

在上面的例子中，英文句子中的"magnet"直译为汉语中的"磁铁"，并增加了"吸引"一词，表明了"硅谷"和"磁铁"之间的共性。再如：

7. "No matter how great the talent or efforts, some things just take time," Mr Buffett said. "You can't produce a baby in one month by getting nine women pregnant."

8. Thousands of neatly stacked and labeled gray boxes of seeds reside in this cavelike structure, forming a sort of backup hard drive, in case natural disasters or human errors erase the seeds from the outside world.

9. "He's wounded, Oliver! Can you just sit there and let your father bleed?" Had she not been in such an emotional state, I could have explained once again that stones do not bleed.

在直译的过程中，我们需要注意直译不能与死译（word-for-word translation）相混淆。茅盾在《"直译"与"意译"》一文中写道："近来颇有人诟病'直译'；他们不是说'看不懂'，就是说'看起来很吃力'。我们以为直译的东西看起来较为吃力，或者有之，却决不会看不懂。看不懂的译文是'死译'的文字，不是直译的。"在直译过程中，译文中除主语和谓语之外的其他句子成分可根据译入语的语言特点在语序和用词等方面进行适当调整。而死译只追求形式上的完全对等，不顾目的语的表达习惯，译文因而也不能表达出原文的意思，是一种硬译，或根本不能称为翻译。请比较下面例子中的直译与死译，并对死译进行修改。

10. I have read your articles. I expected to meet an older man.
死译：我读过你的文章，期望见到一位更老的人。
直译：

11. Many of his ideas are especially interesting to modern youth.
死译：他的许多思想对当代青年特别有趣。
直译：

12. The greatest recent social changes have been in the lives of women.
死译：最大的近年来的社会变革是在妇女生活方面。
直译：

第 2 节 意 译 法

因地理、历史、文化等方面的不同，英语和汉语在词汇、句法结构、表达习惯、修辞手法等方面都有自己不同的特点，在翻译过程中，往往不能直接对应。这时，一味地保持原文的形式只能让译文变得晦涩难懂，因此，在这种情况下，译者应采用意译。例如，"as poor as church mouse" 在翻译时 "church" 和 "mouse" 都不用译出，意译为汉语中表示贫穷的成语 "家徒四壁"；"at sixes and sevens" 不是直译出其中的数字 "six" 和 "seven"，而是根据意思意译为 "乱七八糟"。再如：

1. Adam's apple

2. New brooms sweep clean

3. Chinese tourists are setting out with a deep wallet—more than half claim they will spend RMB 1,000–5,000 yuan, and nearly one fifth will spend over RMB 5,000 yuan, with a large proportion earmarked for retail therapy.

4. Stroll through the farmers' market and you will hear a plethora of languages and see a rainbow of faces.

5. These are home-grown, grass-roots solutions for grass-roots problems—precisely the kind of solutions that Africa needs.

6. I just became 10 times more appreciative of her humility and how humble she was in working with us.

7. US scientists have amassed "planetary-scale" data from people's smartphones to see how active we really are.

使用意译法时，译者在原文形式的把握上比较灵活，但不能任意删减或增加原文的意思，或增加译者的个人感情。要避免过度意译、附加过多的额外信息或改变、歪曲原文的信息。另外，在使用意译法时，译者自身需具备对两种语言精确的把握、扎实的语言知识和深厚的语言功底。请赏析下面两个例子的译文。

7. You can fool all the people some of the time and some of the people all the time, but you cannot fool all the people all the time.

骗人一夕一事易，欺众一生一世难。

8. Out of the fullness of the heart the mouth speaks.

盈于心则溢于言。

第 4 章 直译与意译

第 3 节 直译与意译相结合

直译与意译只是翻译形式的不同,其根本目的都在于为译文读者搭起了解原文的桥梁,忠实、通顺地表达原文的内容。在很多情况下,一句话或一段文字的翻译并不局限于直译或意译。而且,在实际翻译中,也没有绝对的直译和意译,很多时候译者会采用直译和意译相结合的方法。有时候以直译为基础的意译可能更接近原文,能更准确地表达原文的意思。因此,我们不应拘泥于直译和意译这两种不同的翻译形式,而应把重点放在译文意思的表达上。例如:

1. Since it kicked off this year, Chinese people in all regions have been glued to their television.

从今年开播起,全国各地的观众都守在电视机前收看。

在上面的例子中,源于足球比赛开球的"kick off"译为"开播","glued"译为"守在",主要使用了意译法,而句子其他部分则用了直译法。再如:

2. The purpose of a test is to show what you have learned about a subject. The world won't end if you don't pass a test. So don't worry excessively about a single test.

3. In a recent speech, Mariann Fischer Boel, the European agriculture and rural development commissioner, said that the 10 percent target was "not a shot in the dark," but was carefully chosen to encourage a level of growth for the biofuel industry that would not produce undue hardship for Europe's poor.

练习

一、修改下面的句子中所给的译文。

1. Maybe Kino has cut off his head and destroyed himself.
   原译:也许吉纳会割掉自己的脑袋,把自己毁了。
   改译:
2. Do you see any green in my eyes?
   原译:你能看见我眼中的绿色吗?

改译：

3. It was an old and ragged moon.
   原译：这是一个又老又破的月亮。
   改译：

4. Our son must go to school. He must break out of the pot that holds us in.
   原译：我们的儿子一定得进学校，他一定得打破这个把我们关在里面的罐子。
   改译：

5. In the kingdom of blind men the one-eyed man is king.
   原译：在盲人的王国里，独眼人就是王。
   改译：

6. What you are doing is really gild the lily!
   原译：你的所作所为可真是给百合花镀金啊！
   改译：

7. She leaped forward and saw that one was Jim and the other a stranger, with dark shiny fluid leaking from his throat.
   原译：她纵身一跳，便看见一个是吉姆，另一个是陌生人。暗黑的，发亮的液体从他的脖子里往外流。
   改译：

二、翻译下面的句子，注意直译和意译的使用。

1. His novel is a mirror of the times.

2. If we attack quickly, we can nip the enemy's plans in the bud.

3. When Kate graduated from high school, she looked at the world through rose-colored glasses.

4. Barbara was born with a silver spoon in her mouth.

5. Agues come on horse back, but go away on foot.

6. A good conscience is a good pillow.

7. Don't take it too serious. Ignore it as you ignore the last winter.

8. Only 15 years ago, these countries seemed poised to assume leadership of the world economy. Now they are dragging it down.

9. Prices drop because there's too little global demand chasing too much global supply, everything from steel to shoes.

10. And I do not mistrust the future; I do not fear what is ahead. For our problems are large, but our heart is larger. Our challenges are great, but our will is greater. And if our flaws are endless, God's love is truly boundless.

11. Blue-chip companies have yet to take the plunge and still spend only a tiny fraction of their budgets on Internet advertising, but that should be about to change.

12. Better still, farmers can plant biofuel crops on "set aside" fields, land that Europe's agriculture policy would otherwise require to be left fallow.

13. The winter morning was clear as a crystal. The sunrise burned red in a pure sky, the shadow on the rim of the wood-lot was darkly blue, and beyond the white and scintillating fields patches of far off forest hung like smoke.

14. Now, less than two years after Mr. Jobs' death, Ms. Powell Jobs is becoming somewhat less private.

15. Tuition lessons are not the be-all and end-all of life. And a score of 70 for a Chinese paper is definitely not the end of life.

三、翻译下面的文章，注意直译和意译这两种翻译方法的选择。

Venice is a fairy-tale city of island and gondolas, where the canals are lined with wedding cake palaces.

The "Serene Republic" of Venice has a turbulent and fascinating history. As Attila the Hun swept through 5th-century Italy toward trembling Rome, he spread proverbial death and destruction in his path. One particularly unfortunate town was razed to the ground, and its terrified inhabitants fled into the marshes on the shores of the Adriatic. The political climate of the times was so insecure that the population deemed it wisest to remain in the swamps and build their houses on stilts in the water, and so Venice got her start.

The Venice we know today is from a much later era, though an era rich with the accumulated spoils of Crusaders and merchantmen. The wizard like rulers of Renaissance Venice shrewdly—sometimes unscrupulously—parlayed Venice into Mistress of the Adriatic, and the many monuments and palaces erected in those days attest to the profit inherent in such a position.

第 5 章

词义的选择与引申

　　词是能独立运用的最小的语言单位,在翻译过程中,如何确定词义非常重要。只有选择了适当的词义,并在必要时恰如其分地加以引申,才能确保译文的达意。而许多人在翻译时往往机械地在两种语言中寻找对应的词,拘泥于源语和目标语中词在"字面上的一致",或选择某词最常用的词义或自己最熟悉的词义来表达这个词,结果译文往往词不达意或造成误译。第 3 章中我们提到英语中一词多义的现象十分普遍,因而译为汉语时词义的确定需认真理解原文、仔细思考、认真推敲。正确选择恰当的词义是保证译文质量的重要前提。本章将从词义确定的技巧、词的褒贬选择、词的轻重选择和词的具体化、抽象化引申四个方面分析英译汉时词义的选择和引申。

第1节　词义的选择

在选择词义时，我们可以根据词类、学科和语境来确定词义。

1.1　根据词类确定词义

英语中有许多一词多类的现象，即使最简单的英语单词，也会身兼不同的词类。例如，"associate"一词可作动词、名词和形容词。作动词时，其含义为"使发生联系，结交"；作名词时，其含义为"伙伴，同事，关联的实物"；作形容词时，其含义为"副的，联合的"。通过判断词类，可以帮助我们最终确定词的含义。试译下面的句子。

1. Through science we've got the idea of associating progress with the future.

2. Mr. Lin is associate director of the institute.

3. She applied for associate membership last year.

4. A former associate of Mr. Pierce's was among the project's boosters.

5. I only associate with good decent fellows. He associates with all sorts of people.

再如，英语单词"like"可作名词、形容词、动词、介词，副词，而且在不同的词类中其用法和词义都有所不同。请翻译下面的句子，注意"like"词义的选择。

6. Like charges repel; unlike charges attract.

7. He likes French more than English.

8. O my luve's like a red red rose.

9. Like knows like.

1.2 根据学科确定词义

一些单词在不同的学科中会有不同的词义，我们在翻译时要特别注意这一点。例如，我们很熟悉的"eye"一词在不同的学科中应译为不同的词义。在理工类学科中"inspection eye"通常指实验中的检查孔，在体育学科中"hoisting eye"指吊环。我们再来看看"brake"一词在专业领域和日常生活中的不同词义。

1. The driver had ample time to brake or swerve and avoid the woman.

2. The government is determined to put a brake on public spending.

"base"在不同的学科中也有不同的词义。例如：

3. The lathe should be set on a firm base.

4. As we all know, a base reacts with an acid to form a salt.

5. Line *AB* is the base of the triangle *ABC*.

6. He is on the second base.

7. The weary troops marched back to the base.

1.3 根据语境确定词义

英国著名语言学家费斯（Firth）曾说：Each word when used in a new context is a new word. 汉语中也有类似的说法："词本无义，义由境生。"由此可见，语境对于确定词义至关重要。我国现代语言学家胡壮麟把语境分为语篇内部语境、情景语境和文化语境。在翻译非文化词时，前两者尤为重要。

语篇内部语境也就是我们通常说的上下文和搭配。从第3章我们已经了解，英语中不少词汇搭配能力很强，在不同的上下文和搭配中，其词义会有不少变化。如果在翻译时仅依赖于所熟悉的基本意义，不充分考虑上下文因素，不厘清搭配关系，就无法准确把握该词在具体句子中的确切含义。例如：

1. His plane developed engine trouble only seven miles after take-off.

他的飞机起飞后在七英里①处就发生了发动机故障。

2. Scientists are developing new drugs to treat cancer.

科学家们正在研制治疗癌症的新药物。

3. She should have developed her own style instead of copying others.

她应该形成她自己的风格，而不是模仿他人。

4. Until a new theory was developed, they did not have much success.

直到新的理论提出，他们才取得了成功。

5. We must develop the natural substances in our country.

我们必须开发我国的自然资源。

6. Did you ever get the pictures developed?

你把照片冲洗了吗？

在上面的六个句子中，"develop"一词在不同的搭配中译为了不同的词义。再如"cover"一词在下面的句子中也有不同的词义。

7. We covered 400 km in three hours.

8. Do these parking restrictions cover residents as well as visitors?

9. She's covering the American election for BBC television.

10. I'm going to the doctor's tomorrow, so do you think you could cover my shift for me?

11. Will £50 cover your expense?

12. We've got all the exits covered, so they've got no chance of escape.

除了语篇内部语境，理解情景语境对于确定词的含义也是至关重要的。情景语境指语篇产生时周围情况、事件的性质、参与者的关系、时间、地点、方式等。人们头脑中的词义是固定的、有限的，然而词在不同场合、情景中的词义是多变的、无限的。例如：

Diner: Waiter, didn't you hear me say, "Well done"?

Waiter (ignoring the pale pink steak): Yes, sir. Thank you very much, sir.

---

① 1英里=1.609 34米。

第 5 章　词义的选择与引申　　55

It's seldom we get any thanks, sir.

顾客：侍者，你没听到我说："煮熟透"吗？

侍者：（无视淡红色的牛肉）听到了，先生。非常感谢您，先生。我们真是很少得到这样的褒奖。

通过上面的例子，我们可以看出，侍者故意忽视了此情景发生的地点是饭店；参与者之间的关系是顾客与侍者；顾客的语气是质问的，谈论的话题是牛肉等一系列情景因素；侍者把"Well done"理解为日常生活中赞扬某人做得好。根据顾客和侍者不同的情景理解，我们把"Well done"进行了不同的翻译。

下面再看另一个例子：

Poet: Do you think I should put more fire into my poetry?

Editor: No, quite reverse (put it into fire).

第 2 节 词义的褒贬

无论是英语还是汉语中的词汇，除了具有基本含义外，还有内涵的、情感的、联想的等很多方面的意义。而且，语言使用者在具体使用某一词时会受到自己的政治立场、观点、感情、文化差异等的影响，因而会赋予词汇一定的感情色彩。词汇按照感情色彩可分为褒义词、贬义词和中性词。一般来说，汉语词汇的感情色彩较强，褒义词和贬义词所占的比重较大；英语词汇感情色彩较弱，中性词所占比例较大。在翻译中，当原文有明显的褒贬色彩时，我们要保持原文中词的感情色彩，即褒义词翻译成褒义词，贬义词翻译成贬义词。例如：

1. He was a man of high fame.
他是位有名望的人。
2. His notoriety as a rake didn't come until his death.
他作为流氓的恶名是死后才传开的。

在上面的例句中，"fame"和"notoriety"都指人的名声，但前者为褒义词，指好名声，因而译为"名望"，后者为贬义词，指坏名声，因而译为恶名。再如：

3. The boy is appreciated by all his teachers for his carefulness in his homework.

4. In fact, it is his meticulousness that is preventing him from making any progress in his research work.

我们上面提到英语中专用的褒义词或贬义词要比汉语少得多，其褒贬大多要靠上下文才能判定。因而在英译汉时，更多的情况是英语中的中性词根据不同的语境译为汉语中的褒义词或贬义词。例如，在下面的例子中"ambition"及其派生形容词"ambitious"都为中性词，需进行褒贬的选择。

5. *Macbeth* is the story of a Scottish soldier who becomes king but is undone by his own ambition.
《麦克白》讲述的是一个苏格兰士兵当上了国王，却毁于自己的野心的故事。
6. She was a very well educated girl with a lively mind, a girl with ambition.

她是个受过良好教育、思维敏捷、抱负远大的女孩子。

7. But as its cycling program sounds so ambitious, I went there to try it.

但鉴于它自行车出行计划听起来如此高大上,我就去体验了一下。

8. She writes in an ambitious style.

她的文风矫揉造作。

再如,下面例子中的"sensitive"和"future"也需要在不同的上下文中进行褒贬的选择。

9. He's very sensitive about being small, so don't mention it.

10. When I need advice, he is a helpful and sensitive friend.

11. It was mid-August and the subject for discussion was the future of Rommel and his Africa Corps.

12. They predicted the youth would have a bright future.

此外,在特定的语境下英文中的贬义词可译为汉语中的褒义词或中性词,或英文中的褒义词译为汉语中的贬义词。例如,在下面的对话中,佩顿将军看到一个士兵在暴风雪的夜晚还在坚守岗位,因而要给他升职,所以这里的"liar"一词不能译为贬义词"说谎者",而至少要译为中性词。

13. Patton said to him, "Joe, what is your rank?"

He replied, "second lieutenant, sir."

Patton said, "You are a liar, sir. You are now a first lieutenant."

你的话说得不对,(而不是你说谎了)你现在是中尉了。

再如,"jealous, accomplice"二词一般为贬义词,"wise"一般为褒义词,但是在下面的例子中,我们需结合上下文进行具体处理。

14. He is jealous of his own reputation.

15. Jordan said he would keep the MVP trophy but give Scottie the car that accompanies the award. Pippen the accomplice, Jordan the master.

16. We went away as wise as we came.

第 3 节　词义的轻重

除了褒贬之外，我们在词义选择上还需注意轻重问题。用词有分量之分，自古就有。比如"屡战屡败"和"屡败屡战"明显侧重点不同。翻译中，我们同样应注意选词的大小、轻重，选择适合具体语境的恰当表达。例如：

1. John Foster Dulles was an internationalist.

原译：约翰·福斯特·杜勒斯是一个国际主义者。

在上面的例子中，"internationalist"在英语中通常指的是反对孤立主义的人，因而译为汉语中的"国际主义者"明显词义译大了，应改为"国际派"。再如：

2. He told his hearers that if the people were attacked by the policemen, the consequence must fall on the heads of the aggressors.

原译：他对听众说，如果人民受到警察的袭击，其后果一定会落到侵略者的头上。

改译：

3. My military career had been inglorious.

原译：我的军队生活是不光荣的。

改译：

4. She put five dollars into my hand. "You have been a great man today."

原译：她把五美元放在我的手里，并说："你今天真伟大。"

改译：

5. At that time thinking the Reverend Mr. Peters, who was out of employ, a fit person to superintend such an institution, I communicated the project to him.

原译：当时，牧师彼得斯先生正好失业。我想，请他负责办理这个学院是再适当不过的了，于是我便把我的计划告诉了他。

改译：

第 4 节　词义的引申

形象与抽象是两个相互对立、相互依存的概念，翻译时，既可保留源语中原有的特点，也可把抽象和具体相互转化。第 3 章英汉两种语言宏观对比中提到，一般来说，在表达同一含义时，英语倾向于抽象表达，汉语倾向于具体表达。因而，在英译汉时，我们常常会遇见具体化引申的实例。在翻译过程中把源语中抽象的表达用具体的词或词组表达出来，可以消除或降低语言差别给翻译带来的损失，使译文保持与原文同样的效果。例如：

1. Vietnam was his entrée to the new administration.

越南战争是他进入新政府的敲门砖。

在上面例子中，英文句子中的"entrée"一词进行了具体化引申。再如：

2. He waited for her arrival with a frenzied agitation.

3. To Mr. Blevins, like many other students of limited means, every week of going to classes seemed like another week of losing money.

同时，英语中也有不少具体的表达。有些时候，当具体表达的词或词组在汉语中理解困难或不能产生相似的联想时，为了忠实于原文、符合汉语的表达习惯、避免"翻译腔"，我们会把英语中表示具体意义的或具体形象的词或词组进行抽象化处理。例如：

4. China always considers this exchange a two-way street.

中国一贯认为这种交流是相互的。

在上面例子中，英文句子中的"a two-way street"进行了抽象化引申。再如：

5. Every life has its roses and thorns.

6. What is learned in the cradle is carried to the grave.

7. The interest rates have see-sawed between 10 and 15 percent.

8. She has tiptoed into the public sphere, pushing her agenda in education as well as global conservation, nutrition and immigration policy.

通过上述例子，我们可以看到，具体化和抽象化在英译汉时并没有固定的规则或规律，我们需要具体问题具体分析，以保证译文的可读性和生动性。

练习

一、翻译下列句子，注意词义的选择与确定。

1. （1）A trial run is needed before the machine is put into operation.

   （2）An intricate network of the computer system runs this company.

   （3）They are loading the run goods into the hold.

2. （1）It never rains but pours.

   （2）But me no Buts.

   （3）It's anything but bad.

   （4）There is no one of us but wishes to go.

   （5）She left but an hour ago.

3. （1）She interviewed six women who have reached positions of great power and influence.

   （2）Your debt situation is only temporary, and it is within your power to resolve it.

   （3）The Prime Minister has the power to dismiss and appoint senior ministers.

   （4）In 1964 Labour came into power.

   （5）This is a newly-built power plant.

(6) What is the power of this engine?

(7) 64 is the third power of 4.

4. (1) The law of reflection holds good for all surfaces.

(2) In his latest collection of poems readers are confronted with a series of reflections on death.

(3) Inhibition in adulthood seems to be very clearly a reflection of a person's experiences as a child.

5. (1) Government figures understate the problem.

(2) Several leading figures resigned the company.

(3) Most women have to watch their figures.

(4) I could see two figures in the distance.

6. He was a man of integrity, but unfortunately he had a certain reputation. I believe the reputation was not deserved.

7. Her husband was a brave pilot during the Second World War.

8. The reckless driver died in the traffic accident.

9. (1) A good salesman must be aggressive.

(2) Aggressive photographers followed the princess everywhere and flooded the media with photos of her private life.

(3) Aggressive nations threaten world peace.

10. (1) Hans was too obviously flattering the gentleman by saying he was the most courageous man he had ever seen.

(2) Mr. Brown felt greatly flattered when he received the invitation to deliver a lecture.

(3) Equipped with the camera extender known as a selfie stick, occasionally referred to as the wand of narcissism, tourists can now reach for flattering selfies wherever they go.

11. (1) Hong Xiuquan raised the famous rebellion against Qing government.

(2) The Red Army put down the enemy's rebellion.

12. Your guess is as good as mine.

13. Ivanka's regular presence has raised eyebrows because she has no official position.

14. The story of the white-haired girl is one of the saddest.

15. There is a mixture of the tiger and the ape in the character of the imperialists.

16. Hitler's storm troops goose-stepped into power in Furth in 1930.

17. The auto industry jumped in, too. In 2003, Brazilian automakers started producing flex-fuel cars that could run on biofuels.

18. We started thinking about this post-9/11 and on the heels of Hurricane Katrina.

19. If a government is trying to raise financing to invest in new infrastructure, it might find receptive ears in private credit markets.

20. Maybe I'd be less cynical if I lived in Amsterdam, Cologne or any other

city with decent cycling facilities, but as a Londoner, I've learned the hard way to be suspicious whenever politicians promise to do anything bike-friendly.

二、翻译下面的段落，注意"get"及其变体在不同语境中的含义。

I got on horseback within ten minutes after I got your letter. When I got to Canterbury, I got a chaise for town, but I got wet through in rain, and I have got such a cold that I shall not get rid of it in a hurry. I got to the Treasury Board about noon, but first of all got shaved and dressed. I soon got into the secret of getting a memorial before the Board, but I could not get an answer then; however I got intelligence from a messenger that I should get one next morning.

第6章

转译法

　　我们在第3章英汉语言对比中已经提到，英语和汉语分属于两种不同的语系，具有不同的思维习惯和文化背景，因而两种语言在语法和表达习惯上存在很多差异。在英译汉过程中，一些句子可以按照词类对译，但更多的句子由于两种语言的表达方式不同，原文和译文在词类上不能机械地"对号入座"。为了使译文符合汉语的表达习惯，准确表达原文的语义，我们在翻译时就需要进行英语和汉语之间的词类转换。词类转译法是英汉翻译的重要方法和技巧之一，通过把源语中的某一个词由原来的词类转译成目标语中另一词类，能够在保持词汇的基本意义的同时，保证译文的流畅通顺。从理论上讲，英语和汉语中各种词类之间都可以相互转译，在本章里，我们将主要探讨其中主要的、翻译中常见的转译情况。

第 1 节 转译为动词

英语和汉语比较起来，汉语中动词使用量要远远大于英语。英语中的许多词类，如名词、介词、形容词和副词在译为汉语时，往往可以转译为汉语中的动词。

1.1 名词转译为动词

英语作为静态性语言的主要标志是名词优势。根据张韵斐在《现代英语词汇学概论》中的统计数据可知，名词占据了整个英语词汇的 73.6%，形容词占 17.0%，而动词仅占 8.6%。此外，在英语中，名词的使用范围比较广，可以作句子中的许多成分，如主语、宾语、表语、同位语等。英语中名词在数量上优于动词的现象要求我们在汉译时必须进行名词向动词的转译，这种转译有一些方法和原则我们可以遵循。

首先，含有动作意味的英语名词可以转译为汉语动词。英语中有一些词兼有名词和动词两种词性，如"water, house, respect"等，还有一些名词，虽为名词形式，但本身有表示动作的含义，如"memory, sight, proof"等。在翻译这类名词时，我们通常需要把其转译为动词。例如：

1. Ford's first pledge was, "Mr. President, you have my support and my loyalty."

福特一开始就保证说："总统先生，我支持您，并效忠您。"

在上句中"pledge, support, loyalty"都是含有动作意味的名词，在汉译时转译为了动词。再如：

2. A glance through his office window offers a panoramic view of the Washington Monument and the Lincoln Memorial.

3. The international food shortage had a direct impact on Kuwait and other barren desert countries.

4. With the click of a mouse, information from the other end of the globe will be transported to your computer screen at the dizzying speed of seven-and-a-half times around the earth per second.

其次，英语中由动词派生的名词往往在汉译时需要转译为动词。派生是英语中一个重要的构词方法，英语中有许多由动词加上"-ment, -ion,

-ence，-ance"等后缀转换而来的名词，在翻译时往往需要转译为动词。例如：

5. As for Elizabeth, her thoughts were at Pemberley this evening more than the last.

伊丽莎白这天晚上尽想着彭伯利，比头天晚上想得还厉害。

上句选自简·奥斯汀的《傲慢与偏见》，其句子中的主语"thought"一词是由"think"派生的名词，且含有动作意味。在汉译时我们把该句由英语中的物称作主语（her thoughts）转换成了汉语中的人称（Elizabeth）做主语，"thought"一词转译为了动词。再如：

6. Acquiring a language requires exposure to that language.

7. Bali was hit again this year by suicide bombers who killed 19 people in explosions at three restaurants.

8. Last year, research warned that parents' immersion in smartphones has left some neglected children starting primary school unable to hold conversations.

再次，以"-er"或"-or"等后缀结尾的名词在不表示职业或身份时，往往译为动词。以"-er"或"-or"等后缀结尾的名词往往表示某种职业或身份，如"teacher, actor, writer"等。但是在英语中，有时这些词并不表示职业或身份，而是具有较强的动作意味，在译为汉语时往往需转译为动词。例如：

9. He is not a smoker, but his boss is a chain-smoker.

他不抽烟，可他的老板却一支接一支地抽。

在上面例子中，"smoker"和"chain-smoker"都不表达职业，不能译为"吸烟者"和"连锁吸烟者"，因而，在汉译时，我们对其进行了转译处理，译为动词"smoke"的词义。再如：

10. Talking with his son, the old man was the forgiver of the young man's past wrong doings.

11. Napoleon, for these people, was very popular. That is why, still today, there are some enemies of the project.

12. London's mayor, Boris Johnson, is a keen cyclist, who issues policy

papers like "Cycling Revolution."

此外，作为习语主体的名词往往可以转译成动词。英语作为静态性语言，有很多弱化动词加名词组成的习语，例如"have a rest, make an attempt"等。这些习语的主要语义不体现在动词上，而是体现在名词上，这类名词在汉译时往往需要译为动词才符合汉语这一动态语言的特点。

13. The next news bulletin, shorter than usual, made no mention of the demonstration.

下一个新闻节目比通常的短，没有提到游行。

在上面的例子中，"made no mention of"中主要语义由"mention"一词体现，我们把其转译为了动词。再如：

14. After two and a half decades of living out her childhood dream, Goodall made an abrupt career shift, from scientist to conservationist.

15. Vegetable seller Ramiben Waghri took out a loan to buy a solar lantern which she uses to light up her stall at night.

1.2　介词转译为动词

据统计，英语中约有 286 个介词和介词短语；而中文中常用的介词还不到 30 个，甚至不少现、当代汉语语法大家认为，现代汉语，特别是口语中，没有真正的介词。由于英语介词量与汉语介词量严重不匹配，英译汉时，可根据具体语境的需要把英文中的介词转译成汉语中的动词，特别是含有动作意味的介词，如"across, in, on, for, against"等。例如：

1. "Coming!" Away she skimmed over the lawn, up the path, up the steps, across the veranda, and into the porch.

"来啦！"她蹦着跳着地跑了，越过草地，跑上小径，跨上台阶，穿过凉台，进了门廊。

在上句中，英语原文中只有一个谓语动词"skimmed"，而汉语译文中把"up, across, into"等都转译为了动词，汉语译文中有六个动词，符合其动态性语言的特点。再如：

2. In just a few hours, she was due to depart on her first trip to Africa.

3. Each morning, about 450 students travel along 17 school bus routes to 10

elementary schools in this lakeside city at the southern tip of Lake Como.

4. And I will think of the hundreds of babies he must have delivered, who are now in the middle of their own lives and their own stories.

1.3 形容词转译为动词

英语中有许多表示知觉、情感、欲望等心理状态或存在状态的形容词，它们与系动词一起构成复合谓语，如"sure, cautious, angry, ignorant, convinced, aware, afraid, concerned, grateful, worried"等。这些形容词在译为汉语时往往直接转译为动词。例如：

1. But not all are convinced of the benefits of mining.

然而，不是所有人都相信采矿会带来好处。

在上例中，英语句子里表达心理状态的形容词"convinced"转译为了汉语动词"相信"。再如：

2. Some experts are more worried about the potential impact to low-income consumers.

3. But the interested spectator is hardly aware yet how far-reaching the effect is in changing the image of man that science moulds.

4. There were apparently a million ways in which one could do this, and my mother was determined that I should be cautioned against every one of them.

1.4 副词转译为动词

英语副词有时也可以转译为汉语动词。例如：

1. We are through with our test report.

我们的实验报告写完了。

上例中，英语句子中的副词"through"含有动作意味，转译为了汉语中的动词"写完了"。再如：

2. An exhibition of new products is on in Shanghai.

3. When the switch is off, the circuit is open and electricity doesn't go through.

第 2 节 转译为名词

动词和名词是一句话中的主干。虽然汉语为动态性语言，英译汉时也有不少英语其他词类转译为汉语名词的情况。

2.1 动词转译为名词

英语中有些动词是由名词派生或转借而来的（如"characterize, symbolize, design, figure, impress, behave, witness, mean, cost"等），这类动词在英语中用得相当普遍，但在汉语中有时候却很难找到相匹配的动词来翻译。因此，译成汉语时，常常将英语中的这类动词转译为名词或"弱化动词+名词"的形式。例如：

1. As the war progressed, he would symbolize their frustrations, the embodiment of all evils.

随着战争的进行，他将成为他们受挫的象征，成为一切不幸的化身。

在上例中，"symbolize"一词是由名词"symbol"派生的动词，在译为汉语时翻译为了"成为……象征"这种"弱化动词+名词"的形式，符合汉语的表达习惯。再如：

2. Before Jack London, the fiction dealing with the working-class was characterized by sympathy for labor and the underprivileged, but chiefly in the spirit of Christian principles of brotherhood.

3. A well-dressed man, who looked and talked like an American, got into the car.

4. The vegetables look better by this light, and it's cheaper than kerosene and doesn't smell.

此外，在英语被动式句子中，有些动词也可以译成"受（遭）到+名词"或"予（加）以+名词"这种"弱化动词+名词"的形式。例如：

5. Snow was treated very shabbily by the U. S. press and officialdom during the period.

在这期间，斯诺受到了美国新闻界和政界极不公平的待遇。

上例中，英语被动式"be treated by"译为了汉语中"受到……待遇"，其中"待遇"一词为"treat"的名词含义。再如：

6. Satellites, however, must be closely watched, for they are constantly being tugged at by the gravitational attraction of the sun, the moon and the earth.

2.2 其他词类转译为名词

英译汉时，除了将英语中的动词转译为汉语中的名词外，也可以将英语的形容词转译为汉语中的名词。在英语中，当形容词前面加上定冠词"the"表示一类人时，或者某些表示事物特征的形容词作表语时，汉译时需将英语的形容词译成汉语相应的名词。例如：

1. The rescue teams did their best to help the sick and the wounded.

救援队尽最大努力救助病人和伤员。

在上例中，"the sick"和"the wounded"都指一类人，在汉译时被译为了汉语中的"病人"和"伤员"。再如：

2. Television is different from radio in that it sends and receives pictures.

3. Official Moscow is going to object the proposal.

此外，英语副词有时也可以转译成汉语名词。例如：

4. Economically and politically, the criminals have been disenfranchised.

这些罪犯已经被剥夺了政治权利和经济权利。

在上例中，"economically"和"politically"译为汉语中的名词"政治权利"和"经济权利"，更符合汉语的表达习惯。再如：

5. Chemically, the two substances are very similar.

6. We are seeing that books are a respite, particularly for young people who are so busy digitally.

第 3 节 其他词类间的转译

在英译汉时，除了转译为动词和转译为名词之外，还有许多其他词类间的转译，我们要在翻译时不拘泥于源语中词的类别，具体问题具体分析，根据上下文进行灵活处理。例如：

1. A telephone is an absolute necessity for this job.

电话对做这项工作是绝对必需的。

在上例中，英语名词"necessity"转译为了汉语形容词"必需的"，同时"absolute"也进行了随之的词类转换。再如：

2. The pallor of his face indicated that he was seriously ill.

3. The managers exchanged courtesies before getting down to business.

4. Buckley was in a clear minority.

5. He who is subject to temptations tends to err.

6. The thief made a trembling confession of his wrong doing.

我们本章所探讨的转译为狭义概念上的转译，即词类的转译。广义上说，转译还包括句子成分之间的转译、表达方式上的转译、语态上的转译、肯定和否定之间的转译等，针对这些转译，我们会在之后的章节中进行探讨。

练习

一、翻译下列句子，注意转译法在其中的运用。

1. I refused his offer of help.

2. "Did you speak from your own observation," said she, "when you told him that my sister loved him, or merely from my information last spring?"

3. Laser is one of the most sensational developments in recent years, because of its applicability to many fields of science and its adaptability to practical uses.

4. The Government has stated its commitment to a major expansion of pre-school education and wants all children to begin school with a basic foundation in literacy and numeracy.

5. In Europe, the conversion of fields that once grew wheat or barley to biofuel crops like rapeseed is already leading to shortages of the ingredients for making pasta and brewing beer.

6. The presence of the Indians here at the time of Columbus' arrival was sufficient proof of it.

7. The seduction of country life made him forget to return to his home in the city.

8. They took a final look at Iron Mike, still intact in the darkness.

9. South Africa has refused to heed the legitimate appeal of the United Nations for co-operation.

10. ... that we here highly resolve ..., that this nation under God, shall have a new birth of freedom, and that government of the people, by the people, for the people, shall not perish from the earth.

11. Out of all the glorious tales written about U. S. revolution for independence from Britain the fact is hardly known that a black man was the first to die for American independence.

12. The Red Army men struggled ahead, across the snow mountains and through the marshes.

13. Party officials worked long hours on meager food, in cold caves, by dim lamps.

14. The fact that she was able to send a message was a hint. But I had to be cautious.

15. Analysts are unsure if the Brazilian achievement can be replicated in Europe—or anywhere else.

16. More and more English-educated Chinese Singaporean parents are becoming increasingly conscious of the importance for their children to be proficient not only in the all-important English language, but also in Chinese.

17. We are resolved to free the human race from the alleviation of poverty and heal and protect our planet. We are determined to take the bold and transformative steps which are urgently needed to shift the world onto a sustainable and resilient path.

18. In Italy's finicky food culture, food crops have to look good and be of high quality to sell—a drought or undue heat can mean an off year.

19. In Europe, the color white symbolizes purity.

20. Formality has always characterized their relationship.

21. Many college students are good at theorizing and poor in doing practical work.

22. One should be psychologically as well as physically sound.

23. Certainly people in enterprises must be mathematically informed if they are to make wise decisions.

24. Gold is not essentially changed by man's treatment of it.

25. It was officially announced that they agreed on a reply to the Soviet Union.

26. The image must be dimensionally correct.

27. I have the great honor to introduce to you Mr. Black.

28. Have you dialed the right number?

29. The intermittent flashes of lightening made us turn apprehensive glances towards the high way.

30. This communication system is chiefly characterized by its simplicity of operation and the ease with which it can be maintained.

二、翻译下面的段落，注意转译法的运用。

I love the acquaintance of young people; because, in the first place, I don't like to think myself growing old. In the next place, young acquaintances must last longest, if they do last; and then, young men have more virtues than old men; they have more generous sentiments in every respect. I love the young dogs of this age: they have more wit and humor and knowledge of life than we had; but then the dogs are not so good scholars. In my early years I read very hard. It is a sad reflection, but a true one, that I knew almost as much at eighteen as I do now. My judgment, to be sure, was not so good. I remember very well, when I was at Oxford, an old gentlemen said to me, "Young man, ply your book diligently now, and acquire a stock of knowledge; for when years come upon you, you will find that poring upon books will be but an irksome task."

第7章

增 词 法

我国著名译学理论家严复在其所译《天演论》卷首的《译例言》中说过:"至原文词理本深,难于共喻,则当前后引衬,以显其意。凡此经营,皆以为达,为达即所以为信也。"这里的"前后引衬",就是指翻译时所用的增补法。英汉两种语言分属印欧语系和汉藏语系,在词法、句法、修辞等方面有很大的差别,这些差别会造成源语和译入语所传递信息的不对等。根据美国著名翻译理论家尤金·奈达的剩余信息理论,在一般情况下,译文读者的信息能力一般小于原文读者。如果译者进行机械死译,试图把同等的信息量以同样长度的语言结构来表达,那么就会出现信息量过大,超出译文读者信息接收能力的情况。因而,为了使译文难度适合译文读者的信息水平,译者须在文中增加必要的信息。通俗地说,一方面,英语中有许多有其义而无其形的词;另一方面,英语中有许多省略或替换的表达,这些都造成了剩余信息的出现。在汉译时,我们应该为了表达更加清晰,更符合汉语语法特点和中国人的文化背景,增加合适的词语来全面体现原文的思想内容,这就是增词法。英译汉中的增词法一般包括以下四种情况:一是语法上的增补;二是语义上的增补;三是修辞上的增补;四是文化背景增补。

第 1 节　语法上的增补

在语法结构上，我们在第 3 章分析过，英语重替代，汉语喜重复。在出现相同的结构或重复的表达时，英语中常用省略或替代，而汉语不怕重复，因为通过重复可以使表达更加清晰有力。此外，英语中没有量词，概括词使用量较少，而汉语则反之。针对上述英、汉两种语言的差异，我们在英译汉时需要增词。因为这类增词一般不涉及意义和内容，而是为了符合汉语语法习惯，所以我们将之称为语法性增补。

1.1　增加原文省略的部分

在英语中，有些词或词组在出现一次之后，再次出现时常常被省略，以避免重复，而在译为汉语时，则往往需要补充还原，才能使汉语表达完整。例如：

1. I judge I would saw out and leave that night if Dad got drunk enough, and I reckoned he would.

我断定那天晚上我爸要是醉得够厉害的，我就可以锯个洞钻出去，我算计着他是会醉得够呛的。

上面的例子选自马克·吐温的经典作品《哈克贝利·费恩历险记》。原文中"would"一词后面省略了"got drunk enough"，而在汉语译文中为了表达清晰，在句尾增补了"醉得够呛的"。再如：

2. People in this culture don't want to be a burden to their families if they can't contribute.

3. Since the country is a melting pot, it makes perfect sense that their food is too.

另外，在英语里，如果前后并列的两个或多个句子中谓语动词一致，通常会把动词省略，或者只重复介词，以使表达精练。译为汉语时则往往需要重复动词，构成排比式表达。例如：

4. Reading makes a full man; conference a ready man; and writing an exact man.

读书使人充实，讨论使人机智，笔记使人准确。

上面这句话出自英国散文家弗朗西斯·培根的《论读书》，译文出自中国当代翻译家王佐良先生笔下。在原文中,第二句和第三句中都省略了"makes"(原作中为古英语中的"maketh")一词,而译文中"使人"出现了三次,符合汉语表达习惯,读起来也朗朗上口。再如:

5. Not every holiday goes according to plan. Planes can be delayed, hotels overbooked and luggage lost.

6. A fool and his words are soon parted; a man of genius and his money.

此外,"多枝共干"结构是英语中比较常见的现象。在英语文章语句里,为了达到简明扼要的效果,一般避免词语的重复而多使用多枝共干结构,即几个词共有的相同的部分,如几个动词共有一个宾语,几个宾语共享一个动词,几个形容词或介词短语共用一个名词或动词等。译为汉语时,为了使译文清楚明白,通常把共有部分补充译出。例如:

7. One day in February 1926 an unknown American writer walked out of a New York snowstorm and into history.

1926年2月的一天,一位不知名的美国作家走出了纽约的暴风雪,也走进了历史。

在上个例子中,英文中介词"out of"和"into"共有一个动词"walked",汉译时"走"译了两次,以保证译文表达完整。再如:

8. The next time I read a Dickens novel, I will think of him and his military service and his 10 languages.

9. Cultural expression, engagement and understanding are fundamental to a vibrant and healthy society.

1.2 增加原文替代的部分

英语中,特别是在回答句和比较句中,常常对重复部分用"it, that, those"等代词或"do, do so, so, neither, nor, as"等结构进行代替。这些替代部分在译为汉语时往往需要增补。例如:

1. Rebecca: "What! Don't you love him?" Amelia: "Yes, of course, I do."
利蓓加:"怎么?你不爱他?"艾米丽:"我当然爱他。"

上个例子出自英国批判现实主义作家萨克雷的《名利场》。在原文中"do"替代了"love him",而译为汉语时译者对其进行了增补,使表达更加明确。再如：

2. Shall I bring you a dictionary or an encyclopedia? Both, please.

3. I tried not to draw too much hope from the incident, but despite my resolve, I did.

4. When I turned around, John was grinning, expectant, studying my face intently to see if he had pleased me. He had.

1.3 词类增补

英语中没有量词，而汉语中却大量使用量词。英译汉时，需增加量词，表示名词的形状、特征、材料或计量单位等。例如：

1. She bought an electronic iron and two quilts.

她买了一个电熨斗和两床被子。

在上面的例子中，为了符合汉语表达习惯，增加了"个，床"两个量词。再如：

2. A red sun rose slowly from the calm sea.

此外，英语中有些动词或动作名词，译成汉语时常需增加"遍、回、番、一眼"等表示行为、动作的动量词。例如：

3. I had a look at the photo and recognized her at once.

我看了一眼照片，马上就认出了她。

在上面的例子中，"had a look at"中的名词"look"转译为了动词"看"，并在后面增加了动量词"一眼"，表达更加准确、地道。再如：

4. I was extremely worried about her, but this was neither the place nor the time for a lecture or an argument.

此外，英语中虽然也有概括词，但其使用量远远少于汉语。因而在英译汉时，特别是在列举时，可以增加"二人、双方，等方面"等概括词进行总结。例如：

5. Great changes have taken place in industry, agriculture and education in China.

中国在工业、农业和教育等方面都发生了巨大的变化。

在上面的例子中，按汉语表达习惯，增加了"等方面"进行概括，表明中国在各方面都发生了翻天覆地的变化。再如：

6. The thesis summed up the new achievements made in electronic computers, artificial satellites and rockets.

第2节　语义上的增补

因为英语用词简洁，有许多英文中的句子，原文语义完整，但如果对应翻译成汉语，会出现汉语句子不够完整或者语义模糊现象。在这种情况下，翻译时需加一些适当的词语，如增加原文字面上没有而语义上包含的字、词，从语义上做必要的补充或说明。这就是语义性增补。

2.1　增补动词

英语作为静态性语言具有名词优势，汉语作为动态性语言具有动词优势。一般来说，一个英语句子中只会出现一个谓语动词，而一个汉语句子中常有多个谓语动词。英、汉两种语言这种动词量上的巨大差异在英译汉时主要用两种方法来补偿：一种是我们在上一章所讲的转译法，即把英语中的名词、形容词、介词、副词等转译为汉语中的动词；另一种是增加动词，即我们可以在名词前增加动词，以符合汉语动态性语言的表达习惯。例如：

1. It also recommends that foreign aid be more directed toward these problems.
它同时建议，外国援助要更直接用于解决这些问题。

在上面的例子中，我们在"这些问题"之前增加了动词"解决"，译文语义更加完整。再如：

2. Climate change is one of the greatest challenges of our time and its adverse impacts undermine the ability of all countries to achieve sustainable development.

3. It is difficult to conceive—80 years and an incandescent literary career later—the idea of publishing the 26-year-old Hemingway was a big risk.

4. This pretty much describes the strategy of most big online social networks, which over the past few years have concentrated on piling on users rather than worrying about profits.

5. Born in 1963 and a student of medicine at Alexandria, in Egypt, he had the same profile as many of the September hijackers: a middle class background, a good education and a willingness to adopt western habits.

2.2 增补名词

英译汉时,增补名词的情况比较复杂。一般来说,有下面四种情况下可以遵循。

第一,英语中有许多不及物动词或及物动词用作不及物动词的情况,通常在译为汉语时需要在其后增补名词,才能保证译文语义的完整。这类增补的名词就是典型的英语中有其义而无其形的词。请看下面一组含有"wash"一词的句子,我们需要根据不同的上下文,增补适当的名词作其宾语。

1. Be sure to wash before meal.

饭前一定要洗手。

2. Doesn't she wash after getting up?

起床后她难道不洗脸刷牙吗?

3. He sometimes forgets to wash before going to bed.

他有时忘记洗脚/澡就上床睡觉。

再如:

4. Day after day she does the same: washing, sweeping, and cooking.

5. Then Lieutenant Grub launched into the old recruiting routine, "See, save and serve. Hannigan, free tour to all the ports in the world. A fine ship for a home. Three meals a day without charge…You mustn't let such a golden opportunity slip by."

第二,英译汉时,为了语义明确,还经常在形容词前增加名词。例如:

6. He was wrinkled and black, with scant gray hair.

他满脸皱纹,皮肤黝黑,头发灰白稀疏。

在上面的句子中,我们增加了名词"满脸、皮肤",使语义表达清晰,使结构与后面的"头发灰白稀疏"一致,符合汉语表达习惯。再如:

7. He is a complicated man—stubborn, coward and sensitive.

8. Stephen came out of the hot mill into the damp wind and cold wet streets, haggard and worn.

第三,增加范畴词是英译汉中最常见的增加名词的形式。英语中的某些抽象名词或专有名词,若单独译出,有时意思会不够明确,因而译为汉语时通常需要在其后增加"现象、作用、方式、状态、任务、情况、局面"等词予以补充说明,这类词即为范畴词,英语中称为"category words"。例如:

9. Now the main impact of terrorism or disasters is a change in destination.

现在,恐怖主义活动或灾害袭击给旅游业造成的影响无非是改变了旅游的目的地而已。

在上面的例子中,我们在"恐怖主义"后增加了范畴词"活动"以符合汉语表达习惯。再如:

10. Still, he supports the mine and hopes it will provide jobs and stem the rash of suicides, particularly among his peers.

11. There is only one area of agreement in this debate that the existing poverty, employment, and earnings statistics are inadequate for one of their primary applications, measuring the consequences of labor market problem.

第四,在英语具体名词表示抽象意义时,汉译时需要在具体名词后增加合适的名词进行概括或引申,才能表达出原文中的抽象含义。例如:

12. He allowed the father to be overruled by the judge, and declared his own son guilty.

他让法官的职责战胜了父子的私情,而判他儿子有罪。

在上面的例子中,"father"和"judge"是具体名词,但在这里指的是"法官的职责"和"父子的私情",所以我们在汉译时对其进行了语义上的增补。再请看下面例子中"lawyer"一词的词义应该如何处理。

13. Kissinger felt that Rogers was quibbling, but the lawyer in Nixon supported the quibble of a fellow lawyer.

2.3 其他语义上的增补

英译汉时,在语义增补方面,除了上述增加动词和名词以使语义明确、完整之外,还有许多其他形式的语义增补。

首先,为了表达上的生动、形象,英译汉时往往可以增加原文中所暗含的形容词或副词。例如,在翻译"What a day!"一句时,我们可以根据情景增加"热、冷、难熬、幸福、悲惨"等形容词,以表达说话者的心情。再如:

1. With what enthusiasm the Chinese people are studying foreign languages!

中国人正以多么高的热情学习外语啊!

在上面的例子中,我们增加了形容词"高的"来突出中国人学习外语的热情。再如:

2. What a leader he was!

3. After the thunderstorm, the clouds melted away.

其次,虽然整体上英语是形合性语言,汉语是意合性语言,但是在英译汉时有些时候还需增补恰当的连词,以清楚表明句子之间隐含的逻辑关系。如:当主语和谓语之间具有因果关系时,当主语表示未成事实时。例如:

4. His failure to observe the traffic regulations resulted in a serious accident.
他不遵守交通规则,结果导致了一起严重的交通事故。

在上面的例子中,我们增加了连接词"结果",以更清晰地表达句子之间的逻辑关系。再如:

5. At the time of Kennedy's assassination, people thought that a second term would have led either to greatness or to disaster.

再次,英语名词分为可数名词和不可数名词,其中可数名词有单复数的词形变化,而汉语名词没有单复数的词形变化。因此,在英译汉时,为了避免表达啰唆,在很多情况下英语名词复数不必表达出来。但是,在强调复数概念时,英语中的名词复数需通过增加"们,群,各"等词或增加重叠词、数词或其他一些词来表达。例如:

6. The mountains began to throw their long blue shadows over the valley.
群山开始向山谷投下一道道蔚蓝色长影。

在上面的例子中,我们增加了量词"一道道"和"群"来突出句子中复数的概念。再如:

7. Every summer, tourists go to the coastal cities.

8. This week and next, governments, international agencies and nongovernmental organizations are gathering in Mexico City at the World Water Forum.

最后,英语动词有一系列的时态变化,而汉语动词却没有对等的表现形式。一般来说,英语动词的时态在译为汉语时可以不译,以避免生硬的表达。

但是，当原文中强调时间概念或强调过去、现在、将来之间的对比时，需增加表示动词时态的词。例如：

9. We won't retreat; we never have and never will.

我们不会后退，我们从来没有后退过，我们将来也不会后退。

在上面的例子中，英文中通过一般现在时、现在完成时和将来时这三种时态体现了过去、现在和将来之间的对比，而汉语中则增加了"会、过、将"等表达时间概念的词。再如：

10. I was, and remain, grateful for the part he played in my release.

11. I had imagined it to be merely a gesture of affection, but it seems it is to smell the lamb and make sure that it is her own.

第 3 节　修辞上的增补

为了使译文优美、生动或强调说话者的感情、情绪，英译汉时可以增加适当的描述词或语气词。例如：

1. Man, that's really living!

伙计，这才是真正的生活哩！

在上面这个例子的汉语译文中，增加语气词"哩"可表示说话人自信、肯定的口气。

2. Don't take it so seriously. I just make fun of you.

3. I didn't think you would hold me for political ransom, so nakedly, any way.

另外，英译汉时，还可以把英语中的词或词组译为汉语中的成语或两字重叠、四字词语等形式，以使译文更加优美、生动。例如：

4. There has been too much publicity about the case.

那件案子已搞得满城风雨，人人皆知。

在上面的例子中，"publicity"译为了汉语"满城风雨，人人皆知"两个四字成语，表达更加形象、生动。再如：

5. Old people say they can remember when there were so many trees that you couldn't see the sky.

6. These early cars were slow, clumsy, and inefficient.

7. It is altogether a mistake to regard science as dry and difficult—much of it as easy as it is interesting.

第 4 节　文化背景增补

东西方文化背景有很大差异，因而英译汉时，对于英语中一些体现文化背景的词和表达，常常需要增加解释说明，以减轻交际负荷，让汉语读者更好地理解原文。例如：

1. He is a modern Samson.

他是一个现代参孙式的大力士。

在上面的例子中，"Samson"（参孙）是《旧约全书》中的人物，以力大无比而著称，因而在译为汉语时我们进行了文化背景方面的增补，增加了"大力士"一词，以让汉语读者更好地理解这句话的意思。

2. We have enrolled every local Cicero.

3. *The Scarlet Letter* was set in New England in the mid-17th century.

4. Paris and Los Angeles are set to stage the 2024 and 2028 Olympic Games—provided they can agree which should go first, as both want to host in 2024.

练习

一、翻译下列句子，注意增词法的使用。

1. The report says governments, especially in developing countries, should spend at least 1 percent of gross domestic product on water and sanitation.

2. A group of Americans are trying to save the house and its contents. Yet the US government won't let them.

3. Histories make men wise; poets witty; the mathematics subtle; natural philosophy deep; moral grave; logic and rhetoric able to contend.

4. Reading exercises one's eyes; speaking one's tongue; while writing, one's mind.

5. A changing climate presents new opportunities, but it also threatens their environment, the stability of their homes, and, for those whose traditions rely on the

第 7 章　增词法　　87

ice-bound wilderness, the preservation of their culture.

6. For the purpose of attaining freedom in the world of nature, man must use natural science to understand, conquer and change nature.

7. I can say to you, without any flattery, that the Chinese way of co-operations is more inventive and fruitful than others.

8. He did not really represent their opinions to the higher-ups, although he claimed he did.

9. Yes, I like Chinese food. Lots of people do these days, sort of the fashion.

10. A stream was winding its way through the valley into the river.

11. Once they quarreled bitterly.

12. The oil, gas and water were always together.

13. China is willing to exchange views with any countries, politically, culturally and economically.

14. Men need to meet up face-to-face and bond over activities, while for female friendships, long phone conversations can bridge the physical distance.

15. For all the natural and man-made disasters of the past year, travelers seem more determined than ever to leave home.

16. Cultural expression expands individual capacities, helps bind society and provides jobs and innovation in the economy.

17. The purpose of engineering is to create useful goods, to make them better, cheaper, and more abundant.

18. Ireland enacted a series of liberal economic policies that resulted in rapid economic growth, coupled with a dramatic rise in inequality.

19. He felt the patriot rise within his breast.

20. The growing demand for quality pre-school and daycare is creating new business opportunities.

21. Now and then his boots shone.

22. The other procedures were workable; however, the costs of generating energy made them uneconomical when compared with methods in general use.

23. There were rows of houses which he had never seen before.

24. Hundreds—perhaps thousands—of lasers are performing useful production functions in the very real world of industry.

25. Mother insisted to this day that she thought I was just joking.

26. Man, was, is and always will be trying to improve his living conditions.

27. I remembered thinking, "No, no. It's not Jackson; it's not my husband; it's not my Jackson. But it is."

28. Their "May-December" marriage ended in a stormy divorce.

29. On one of our first Christmases together, my husband gave me a complete set of Dickens.

30. The blond boy quickly crossed himself.

二、翻译下面的段落,注意增词法的使用。

It is frequently said that computers solve problems only because they are "programmed" to do so. They can only do what men have them do. One must remember that human beings also can only do what they are "programmed" to do. Our genes "program" us the instant the fertilized ovum is formed, and our potentialities are limited by that "program."

Our "program" is so much more enormously complex, though, that we might like to define "thinking" in terms of the creativity that goes into writing a great play or composing a great symphony, into developing a brilliant scientific theory or a profound moral judgment. In that sense, computers certainly can't think and neither can most humans.

第8章

减 词 法

　　增词法和减词法是英汉翻译中两种相辅相成的翻译方法和技巧。张泽乾教授曾指出"增译、减译都要适合语法、语义、修辞的需要。增只能增原文形式之所无，减必须保持原文内容之所有。或增或减、有增有减均应无伤大雅，无损原意"。减词法，也可以称为"省略法"、"省译法"或"减省法"，是指在翻译过程中将原文的一些词省略不译，这些词往往是不符合译入语思维习惯、语言习惯和表达方式的词，包括无用的词、意思重复的词等，以避免译文表达累赘。如张泽乾教授所述，减词法的最根本原则是"减词不减意"，也就是说，在不改变原文意思的前提下，省略一些译文中可有可无的词，避免"翻译腔"，使译文更加简练、表达流畅自然。英译汉中的减词法主要包括语法上的减省和修辞上的减省两个方面。

第 1 节　语法上的减省

在语法方面，英、汉两种语言在词的类别和不同词类的使用频率上有很大差别。英语中有冠词，汉语中没有冠词；英语代词使用频率高，汉语中代词的使用频度明显较低；英语中多用介词，汉语则多用动词表达介词之意或干脆不用介词；英语为形合性语言，各种连接词必不可省，而汉语为意合性语言，句子多为板块结构，连接词能省则省。综上所述，英译汉时，语法性减省需要省译英语有而汉语中没有的词类（如冠词）或英语用得多而汉语用得少的词类（如代词、介词、连词等）。

1.1　省译冠词

冠词是英语中特有的一种词性。尽管英语中只有"a, an, the"三个冠词，但它们的用途很广、用法复杂。英译汉时，我们应当注意区分冠词是起语法作用，还是表达某种实际的意义。对于只起语法作用、不表达实际意义的冠词，我们在翻译中应当减省。例如：

1. A CEO should have ambition.

总裁应当有雄心。

在上面的例子中，"a CEO"指的是一类人而不是一个人，因而不定冠词"a"进行了省译。再如：

2. Years ago, to fly to the moon was out of the question.

3. The policeman asked the driver to describe the accident in greater detail.

但是，当冠词表达实际意义，如不定冠词表达数量、定冠词表达特指时，不能省译。例如：

4. The taxi driver said that he was getting a dollar a mile.

出租汽车司机说他每开一英里可赚一美元。

在上面的例子中，两个不定冠词"a"表达的都是数量，所以不能省译。再如：

5. He had been patiently waiting in the anteroom for an hour.

6. The traveler saw the bird fly away.

1.2　省译代词

代词在英语中的使用非常普遍。英语中一般大量使用人称代词、物主代词、反身代词、代词"it"等各种代词形式,在一篇英语文章中,代词会占到较大的比率;而汉语中则一般避免使用过多的代词,甚至一篇一二百字的汉语文章,没有代词也不罕见。现代汉语语言学家王力先生曾指出汉语中代词的使用原则是"若要明白,不如名词复说;若要简洁,不如索性不用"。英译汉时,在保证表达清楚的前提下,我们可省译各种不必要的代词,以符合汉语的表达习惯。例如:

1. As we discuss our differences, neither of us will compromise our principles. But while we cannot close the gulf between us, we can try to bridge it so that we may be able to talk across it.

原译:在我们讨论我们的分歧的时候,我们哪一方都不会在我们的原则问题上妥协。虽然我们不能弥合我们之间的鸿沟,但是我们能设法搭一座桥,以便越过它进行会谈。

在上面的例子中,原文中有 37 个单词,其中代词 10 个,几乎占了原文词量的三分之一。在汉语原译中,全部保留了这 10 个代词,但译文显得十分啰唆、拗口,需要对里面不必要的代词进行省译。

改译:在讨论我们的分歧时,哪一方都不会在原则问题上妥协,虽然不能弥合我们之间的鸿沟,但是我们能设法搭一座桥,以便越过它进行会谈。

省译代词的情况比较复杂。一般来说,人称代词在作主语和作宾语时,如果前面已经提及,经常需要省译。例如:

2. But it's the way I am, and try as I might, I haven't been able to change it.

3. He was thin and haggard and he looked miserable.

4. The Beatles—I never get tired of listening to them.

此外,英语人称代词作主语表泛指时,即使是作第一个主语,译为汉语时也需减省,即译为汉语的无主句。例如:

5. He who made the mistake should have the courage to admit.

6. You are kindly requested to let us have your best quotation for the canned fish.

英语中物主代词的使用十分频繁。凡是属于某人的或和某人相关的，都需要使用适当的物主代词，而汉译时一般需省略。例如：

7. He entered into the room, his coat covered with snow and his nose red with cold.

8. For two weeks, he had been studying the house, looking at its rooms, its electric wiring, its path and its garden.

英语中的反身代词译为汉语时也常常省译。例如：
9. We sat round the fire to keep ourselves warm.

10. Scientists have to train themselves to use their brain efficiently.

代词"it"在英语中有许多用法，可以作第三人称主语、宾语，可以表示时间、天气，可以引导强调句型，还可以作形式主语或形式宾语。在英译汉时，"it"常常可以省译。例如：
11. Antonia will not be jealous, or if she is, she will not show it.
安东尼娅不会嫉妒，即便嫉妒，她也不会表现出来。
上句中，"it"作宾语，指代"嫉妒"，因为前面已经提到，因而需省译。再如：
12. It was very wet and windy the day I drove over the hill to Milland.

13. It was in this mountain that this rare kind of plant was found.

14. This formula makes it easy to determine the wavelength of sounds.

15. It was noted that within a year the incidence of illness had increased quite significantly.

另外，定语从句、名词性从句中的关系代词/副词、连接代词在英译汉中往往也可省译，我们之后会对其详加探讨。

1.3 省译连词

英语句子讲究形式上的严谨，句子内部的逻辑关系主要依靠连词来体现，而汉语句子注重的是意思的连贯，句子内部的逻辑关系往往是暗含的或由先后顺序决定的，在很多情况下不一定需要连接词。因此，在英译汉时英语中的连词并非都要译出，适当地省译连接词可以使译文更加简洁，读起来节奏感强、朗朗上口。例如：

1. Promote physical culture and build up the people's health.

发展体育运动，增强人民体质。

在上面的例子中，我们省译了并列连词"and"，译文读起来朗朗上口，符合汉语表达习惯。再如：

2. Some bacteria are exceedingly harmful but others are very helpful.

3. The gap between the rich and the poor is the product of complex forces, and won't be fixed overnight.

在上面的例子中，我们可以看到，并列连词"and, but"等一般可以省译。同样，从属连词在英译汉时也可以省译，但有时需要调整语序。例如：

4. Practically all substances expand when heated and contract when cooled.

实际上一切物质都是热胀冷缩的

在上面的例子中，我们省译了连词"when"，把英文中的复合句压缩为了汉语中的简单句，译文简洁明了。

5. If a body moved from one position to another, it is said to have had displacement.

6. The average speed of all molecules remains the same, as long as the temperature is constant.

1.4 省译介词

第6章我们提到过，英语中的介词量几乎是汉语中的十倍。为了弥合英、汉两种语言中这种巨大的差异，英译汉时，除了一些介词可以转译为动词外，还有不少介词可以省译。特别是一些表示时间或地点的介词短语在译文句首时，通常可以省译。例如：

第 8 章 减词法 95

1. They will make an experiment on physics.
他们将做物理实验。
在上面的例子中，省译了介词"on"，符合汉语表达习惯。再如：
2. The products produced in this factory are good in quality and low in price.

3. An ancient castle stood on the edge of the cliff.

4. She remained silent with her head down all the time.

5. Regarding marriage, I have my own way.

1.5 省译动词

英语中只有动词才能作谓语，而汉语中可以直接用数词、形容词、副词、名词、主谓短语等形式作谓语。因而，在不影响完整表达原文内容的前提下，汉语译文常省译系动词。例如：
1. He was sixty-eight. In two years he would be seventy.
他 68 岁，再过两年就 70 了。
在上句中，系动词"was, be"主要起语法连接作用，需要省译。再如：
2. When the pressure gets low, the boiling point becomes low.

3. As Hugh grew older, she had less influence and couldn't control him.

有时，英语中的一些实义动词，特别是在句子中不承担主要意思的实义动词，在汉译时也可以省译。例如：
4. This laser beam covers a very narrow range of frequencies.
这种激光束的频率范围很窄。
在上面的例子中，"cover"不表达主要语义，因而在译文中进行了省译，选择"范围很窄"这一主谓结构作谓语更符合汉语表达习惯。再如：
5. For this reason television signals have a short range.

6. Stainless steels possess good hardness and high strength.

7. In mid-1977, world sea-going tonnage amounted to 338.5 million grt which reflects a rise of 5.8% in grt over mid-1976, compared with a corresponding increase of 9% from mid-1975 to mid-1976.

第 2 节　修辞上的减省

修辞上的减省是指从修辞角度考虑,省略原文中一些成分,使译文简洁明了,避免表达累赘、啰唆。这些所省译词语的含义在译文中虽然没有明确译出,但已暗含在其中,因此不会影响对原文整体意思的传递。

2.1　省译重复的词或词组

英语中习惯用同义词或近义词表达同一概念或意义。在这种情况下,我们在译为汉语时,通常把二者的语义缩译或直接省译其一。例如:

1. The mechanical energy can be changed back into electrical energy by means of a generator or dynamo.

利用发电机能把机械能转变为电能。

在上面的例子中,"generator" 和 "dynamo" 同为 "发电机" 之意,所以只译出一词便可。再如:

2. The contract is null and void because of violations.

3. He hopes that he may once again repeat, upon a greater scale than ever before, that process of destroying his enemies one by one which he has so long thrived and prospered.

另外,英语中重复的表达在译为汉语时也可省译,例如:

4. The problem of alternative fuels of vehicle is one problem we shall approach.

车辆的代用燃料是我们将要着手处理的一个问题。

在上例中,"problem" 一词重复了两次,我们可以省译一次,以避免译文表达啰唆。再如:

5. She curtseyed again, and would have blushed deeper, if she could have blushed deeper than she has blushed all the time.

2.2　省译不言而喻的词

有些词或词组在英语中必不可少,但在汉语中其语义往往是不言而喻的,因而,译为汉语时可以省去或精简,以达到译文简洁流畅、"文约而意丰" 的效果。例如:

1. The capital and largest city is Dublin, whose metropolitan area is home to around a quarter of the country's 4.6 million inhabitants.

首都都柏林是最大的城市，人口约为全国 460 万人口的 1/4。

在上面的例子中，我们省译了"whose metropolitan area"，因为前面已经提到了"首都都柏林是最大的城市"，人口指都柏林的市区人口是不言而喻的。再如：

2. France is set to ban the sale of any car that uses petrol or diesel fuel by 2040.

3. There are some things that I have happily seen of the wondrous way of the spider.

4. To learn is not an easy matter and to apply what one has learned is even harder.

5. The new prime minister, David Cameron, has reversed many of his predecessor's promises as part of a program to cut more than £99 billion annually over the next five years to help close a gaping budget deficit.

练习

一、翻译下列句子，注意减词法的使用。

1. My profession had an important influence on the formation of my character and temperament.

2. An area in which the computer has made considerable strides in recent years is in playing chess.

3. The teacher should encourage the child to proceed as far as he can, and when he is stuck, ask for help.

4. The significance of a man is not in what he attains but rather in what he longs to attain.

5. We assure you of our prompt attention to this matter.

6. They wanted to determine if he complied with the terms of his employment and his obligations as an American.

7. He shrugged his shoulders, shook his head, cast upon his eyes, but said nothing.

8. The train came. He pinched his little sister lovingly, and put his great arms about his mother's neck and then was away.

9. They have to wear special clothes in order to keep themselves warm.

10. It is really the poor countries that don't have an economic base that have the worst environmental records.

11. He found it hard to work with a microphone pointing at him.

12. We're at a critical moment and if we don't act fast, we're going to lose a lot of plants that we may need.

13. It has long been believed that the smartphones in our pockets are actually making us dumber; but now there is evidence for it.

14. When at last he stood upon the bluff, he turned to his little sister and looked upon her sorrowfully.

15. Because the departure was not easy, we'd better make it brief.

16. We knew spring was coming as we had seen a robin.

17. She has worked hard at her marriage.

18. He grew tired, and drifted off into a drugged sleep.

19. These developing countries cover vast territories, encompass a large population and abound in natural resources.

20. People use money to buy all kinds of things they need or want.

21. Scientists believed that disruption to the body's natural body clock was responsible for the increased risk of chronic illness.

22. He used to lend money to people in distress, and would never take any interest for the money he lent.

23. Standing as it does on a high hill, the church commands a new view.

24. Part-time waitress applicants who had worked at a job would receive preference over those who had not.

25. John sat near her on the bed. His face was white as he sat holding her hot hands.

二、翻译下面的段落，注意减词法的使用。

Most Americans have great vigor and enthusiasm. They prefer to discipline themselves rather than be disciplined by others. They pride themselves on their independence, their right to make up their own minds. They are prepared to take the initiative, even when there is a risk in doing so. They have courage and do not give in easily. They will take any sort of job anywhere rather than be unemployed. The average American changes his or her job nine or ten times during his or her working life.

Americans have a warmth and friendliness which is less superficial than many foreigners think. They are considered sentimental. When on ceremonial occasions they see a flag, or attend parades celebrating America's glorious past, tears may come to their eyes. Reunions with family and friends tend to be emotional, too. They love to boast, though often with tongue in cheek. They can laugh at themselves and their country, and they can be very self-critical, while remaining always intensely patriotic. They have a wide knowledge of everyday things, and a keen interest in their particular city and state. Foreigners sometimes complain, however, that they have little interest in or knowledge of the outside world.

第9章 正反译法

英语和汉语中均有从正面或反面来表达思想的现象，但由于中西方不同的社会文化、生活方式和风俗习惯，在语言上，同一问题、同一概念，会出现不同的正、反表达方式。英语词句中含有"no, not, none, never, nothing, nobody, nowhere, neither"等完全否定词，"hardly, scarcely, seldom, barely, few, little"等半否定词或"de-, dis-, in-, im-, un-, ir-, non-, -less"等否定前缀或后缀，汉语词句中含有"不、没、无、未、休、莫、非、勿"等成分的为反说，不含有这些成分的为正说。英语里有些用肯定语气表达的词或句子，在汉语译文中可以从反面（用否定语气）来表达；英语里用否定语气表达的词或句子，在汉语译文中也可以从正面（用肯定语气）来表达。我们在翻译时要根据语境特点，充分利用正说反译和反说正译的方法，使译文符合汉语习惯。同时我们还需要注意，正说反译和反说正译只是表达方式的不同，而不是对原文意思的正反改变。

第 1 节　正 说 反 译

英语中有不少"含蓄否定"或"暗指否定"词或词组,如"fail, ignore, refuse, safely, idly, thin, narrow, above, beyond, but for, before, rather than, far from, keep from"等。从词形上看,这类词是肯定式;从词义上看,它们大多数是某些词的反义词。通过长期的历史演变,这些曾完全作为反义词用的词义又引申出其他含有否定意义的词义。这类词在译为汉语时往往需要译为否定词或词组,有时还需进行词类转换。例如:

1. I regret to learn that you have failed in the examination.

得知你未能通过考试,我很遗憾。

在上句中,"failed"一词形式上是肯定的,即正说,但因为其含有否定的意思,我们进行了反译。再如:

2. Undergraduates will tell you that they're under pressure—from their parents, from the burden of debt they incur, from society at large—to choose majors they believe will lead as directly as possible to good jobs. Too often, that means skipping the humanities.

3. Tuition bills scare some students from even applying and leave others with years of debt.

4. Most European countries are far from achieving the target, and are introducing incentives and subsidies to bolster production.

5. Many high schools do a poor job of preparing teenagers for college.

6. He dived into the water fully clothed and rescued the children.

7. I stayed awake almost the whole night. I'll be here for good this time.

8. In countries that have trouble delivering clean water to their people, a lack of infrastructure is often the culprit.

9. Each morning, about 450 students travel along 17 school bus routes to 10

elementary schools in this lakeside city at the southern tip of Lake Como. There are zero school buses.

10. We lived beyond our means.

11. The lecture was interesting, but as far as I am concerned the speaker was speaking over my head.

12. Before I could say "thank you," the postman had disappeared around the corner.

13. Life may well turn out to be the rule, rather than exception.

不仅上面例子中的英语动词、形容词、副词、名词、介词、连词等各种词类汉译时可以采用正说反译法，英语中的一些固定短语或句子也需要进行正说反译。例如：

14. The escaped criminal is still at large.
逃犯仍未捉拿归案。

在上面的例子中，词组"at large"译为了"未捉拿归案"这一否定形式的表达。再如：

15. The hotel was anything but satisfactory.

16. This actress is already 60, but she carries her years lightly.

17. Usually we go down the middle. That way, everybody gets a shot at us.

此外，英语中的谚语、警句或公示语等习惯以肯定的方式进行告知，而汉语则习惯以否定的形式进行告诫，因此，在英译汉时，也需正说反译。

18. Good winner, good loser.
胜不骄，败不馁。

在上例中，英文句子告诉人们要成为"Good winner, good loser"，而根据汉语告诫的表达习惯，我们对其进行了反译。再如：

19. Adults only.

20. Staff only.

21. Keep upright.

第 2 节　反 说 正 译

英语中有些与否定词连用的词语或带有否定前缀或后缀的词语，有时可以译成汉语的肯定形式，以使语义清楚明了，使译文自然流畅，符合汉语表达习惯。以《哈姆雷特》中最著名的 "To be or not to be, that is the question." 为例，"not to be" 译为汉语时没有采用原来的否定形式，而是译为了"死"，即 "to be（生）" 的反义词，这样译更符合汉语表达习惯。再如：

1. The dishonesty of the city officials was exposed by the newspaper.

2. Bill is too indecisive to make a good leader.

3. It is invariably wet when I take my holidays.

4. The boss could fire any employee who had ever displeased him.

5. He returned home with no hope on his face.

第3节 双重否定句

双重否定句是英语中常见的一种句式，有时可以译成汉语中的双重否定句，有时可以译成汉语中的肯定句，具体情况应视语气、习惯表达法、修辞效果和逻辑等而定。一般来说，英语中的双重否定句常译为汉语中的肯定句。例如：

1. They never meet without quarrelling.

他们一见面就争吵不休。

在上面的例子中，英语中的双重否定句译为了汉语中的肯定句，表达了一种无可置疑的语气，因而大大增强了效果。再如：

2. The charging of a condenser from a battery is not unlike the filling of a tank from an oil reservoir.

3. To make both ends meet it is not uncommon for teachers in America to take second jobs in the evening and in their summer holidays.

有时，英语中的双重否定句也可以译为汉语中的否定句，一般表达委婉语气，起到一种缓和效果的作用。例如：

4. No smoke without fire.

无风不起浪。

在上例中，我们保留了英语双重否定句的形式，更符合汉语表达习惯。再如：

5. He will not do it for nothing.

6. Not a student has access to the library without showing his student card.

此外，英语中还经常出现否定词加上含有否定意义的词构成双重否定句的形式，我们在译为汉语时需特别注意。例如：

7. Such mistakes couldn't long escape notice.

这类错误迟早会被发觉的。

在这个例子中，"couldn't"和"escape"组成了英语中暗含的双重否定句，其中"escape"为含有否定意义的词。再如：

8. We must never stop taking an optimistic view of life.

9. The thought of returning to his native land never deserted him amid his tribulations.

第 4 节 否 定 陷 阱

英语中有一些特殊的否定形式，如转移式否定、部分否定、强调式双重否定等，需要我们在翻译时特别小心，以免掉入否定"陷阱"。

4.1 部分否定

在英语中"all/ every/ both...not"结构中，无论 not 的位置如何，一般都表达一种部分否定，而不是全部否定。例如：

1. All's not smooth for Lakers.
"湖人队"未必一帆风顺。

2. All glitters is not gold.

3. Both of the substances do not dissolve in water.

4.2 转移式否定

一般来说，句子中的"not"等否定词通常否定谓语，但有时，也可以表示否定的转移，用来否定句子中的其他成分。例如：

1. The engine didn't stop because the fuel was finished.
发动机并不是因为燃料耗尽而停止运转的。

在上例中，如果我们把"not"译为否定谓语"stop"，原文则不符合逻辑。这里，对"not"进行了否定转移，让其修饰"because"所引导的原因状语更符合汉语表达习惯。再如：

2. In South Carolina we had never suffered discrimination because we were Jews.

3. My honorable friend and I will not be going to Moscow to conduct negotiation on behalf of the west.

4. We are not here to interfere, nor are we here to be anyone's whipping boy.

4.3 强调式双重否定

在古英语或现代英语口语中，有时句子中的两个否定词之间在意义上并不总是互相抵消，形成强调式的肯定，而是其中一个否定词是对另一个否定词在否定意义上的强调，表示强调式否定。例如：

1. I don't know nothing about what's waiting for me.

我不知道我未来命运如何。

2. He didn't tolerate no opposition from the politicians.

3. I worked and worked, and I didn't know how much I had not done.

4.4 其他否定陷阱

除了上面我们提到的特殊否定形式外，英语中还有不少其他否定陷阱，我们在翻译时需特别留意。

例如"cannot...too"的意思一般不是"不能太……"，而是"无论……也不过分"。它还有几个变体的结构：用"impossible, difficult"等词代替"cannot"；以"sufficiently, exaggerate, enough"等词替代"too"。请看下面的例子。

1. The importance of agriculture cannot be overstated.

农业的重要性怎样强调都不为过。

2. A book may be compared to your neighbour; if it is good, it can not last too long; if bad, you cannot get rid of it too early.

3. Young scientists cannot realize too soon that existing scientific knowledge is not nearly so complete, certain and unalterable as many textbooks seem to imply.

再如"for all..."表面看是一种肯定的表达，但它往往含有否定之意。请看下面的例子：

4. You can go right now for all I care.

5. Richard Nixon sent me alone, cut off from communications. For all he knew, I was going to sell Alaska.

此外，英语中的"It be+*adj.* +*n.* +that"结构一般用来表示一些比较有哲理的句子。因为不同的表达习惯，它被译为汉语时往往有"再……也难免"之意。例如：

6. It's a long lane that has no turning.

7. It is a good workman that never blunders.

8. It is a wise father that knows his own child.

练习

一、修改下列句子，注意正反译法的使用。

1. John was a fool for danger.
   原译：约翰对危险是傻子。
   改译：

2. Such a chance was denied me.
   原译：我被这样一个机会拒绝了。
   改译：

3. I deserve it. I deserve that they should know. I am too silly to be alive.
   原译：真是的！我应该让他们知道这件事。我傻得不能活。
   改译：

4. The research group lost no time in carrying out their new plan.
   原译：研究小组不失时间地执行了他们的新计划。
   改译：

5. If we can help you further, please don't hesitate to get in touch with us.
   原译：愿意为你们进一步服务，如有需要，请与我们联系，请勿犹豫。
   改译：

6. We are not completely satisfied with your manner of doing business.
   原译：我们不十分满意贵方做生意的态度。
   改译：

7. If you forward the transcripts yourself, they can be considered official only if the school envelope has remained sealed.
   原译：如果你本人递交证件，只有校方信封保持密封，才可被认为是正式的。
   改译：

8. Plastics for industrial purposes are not valuable because they are colorful.
   原译：工业用的塑料没有价值，因为它们是五颜六色的。

改译：

9. Africa is not kicking out Western imperialism in order to invite other new masters.

原译：非洲不踢出西方帝国主义为了请进其他新的主子。

改译：

10. I believe then that I would die there, and I saw with a terrible clarity the things of the valley below. They were not the less beautiful to me.

原译：这时我觉得我要死在那儿了，而下面山谷里的景致却看得异常清晰。在我看来，这些景致并没有减少美丽。

改译：

二、翻译下列句子，注意正反译法的使用。

1. But she began declining interviews in the mid-1960s and, until late in her life, firmly avoided making any public comment about her novel or her career.

2. Please remain seated until the aircraft comes to a complete stop.

3. Professor White is an outstanding physicist, but as a teacher he leaves much to be desired.

4. The humanities often do a bad job of explaining why the humanities matter.

5. In a system committed to the health of farms and their integration with local communities, the result would have been different.

6. Slowly he pulled the letter out of the envelope, and unfolded it.

7. There was complete absence of information on the oil deposit in this area.

8. He spoke English very well; except for a slight accent you'd never have known that he was a foreigner.

9. And somehow, the volunteers just kept coming.

10. It was beyond his power to sign such a contract.

11. Only one of them has ever gone to live in the country and he was back in town within six months.

12. Now is the time for the industry to act before there is major outcry.

13. There are many energy sources in store. The problem has been to use the energy at a reasonable cost.

14. I am wiser than to believe such stories.

15. Wet paint.

16. It always takes two.

17. The examination left no doubt that the patient had died of cancer.

18. Everyone felt nervous that afternoon, and they all went about their work in an unusually careful manner.

19. Yesterday the President gave unprepared speech before a big audience.

20. Even to this day they never hear a thunder-storm of a summer afternoon about the Keatskill, but they say Hendrick Hudson and his crew are at their games of ninepins.

21. Gertrude Stein had no interest in anything that was not aggressively modern.

22. You cannot make egg rolls without breaking eggs.

23. I never read novels that don't appeal to me.

24. This fresh air will do you no harm after you being in the house all day.

25. I have not come to China to forth on what divides us but to build on what

binds us.

26. Both of the instruments are not precision ones.

27. Once Mrs. Grand asked him something about Stalin and his reply was, "May, I don't write no social column."

28. These scientists could not believe the two Curies more.

29. For all I care, you can throw it away.

30. It's an ill wind that blows nobody good.

三、翻译下面的段落,注意正反译法的使用。

Some people think that it is a shame that a censor should interfere with works of art. But we must bear in mind that the great proportion of books, plays and films which come before the censor are very far from being "works of art." When censorship laws are relaxed, dishonest people are given a chance to produce virtually anything in the name of "art." One of the great things that censorship does is to prevent certain people from making fat profits by corrupting the minds of others. To argue in favour of absolute freedom is to argue in favour of anarchy. Society would really be the better if it were protected by correct censorship.

第10章

语序调整

　　语序是语言的重要组合手段之一，反映一定的逻辑事理以及语言使用者的语言习惯和思维模式。中英文描述同一客观事实有不同的语言表达顺序，因而语序调整是英译汉中一个重要的翻译方法。本章主要从词序调整和句序调整两个方面探讨英译汉时的语序调整。

第 1 节　词 序 调 整

第 3 章在英汉两种语言的微观对比中，我们已经探讨了英、汉在定语和状语层面的词序不同，在这里我们不再赘述。除此之外，英语和汉语中许多并列成分在词序方面也不尽相同，例如莎士比亚在其第 105 首十四行诗中写到 "Fair, kind and true, is all my argument"，而汉语中针对 "fair, kind and true" 三个词的顺序则习惯是 "真、善、美"。一般来说，英语中并列的词序按照逻辑上的轻重、前后、因果或从部分到整体的顺序安排，而汉语通常则将较大、较强、较突出或给人印象较深的成分前置。例如：

1. iron and steel industry 钢铁工业

在上面的例子中，将 "iron" 和 "steel" 译为汉语时，根据汉语表达习惯对其进行了词序调整。再如：

2. elementary and high school

3. in twos and threes

4. flesh-and-blood characters

5. heal the wounded and rescue the dying

6. land and water communication

第 2 节 句 序 调 整

英语是形合性语言，句子之间的关系主要由连接词决定，而汉语是意合性语言，句子之间的关系主要由先后顺序或内在的逻辑关系决定。因而，英译汉时，我们主要从时间顺序和逻辑顺序两个方面考虑句子之间语序的调整。

2.1 时间顺序

英语句子是树形结构的，句子成分叠床架屋，形成一个立体的空间构架，时间顺序一般显示不出来。汉语句子是板块结构的，各分句疏散铺排，时间顺序一般表现得比较清晰。例如：

1. I put on my clothes by the light of a half-moon just setting, whose rays streamed through the narrow window near my crib.

原句包含三个分句：① I put on my clothes by the light of a half-moon. ② A half-moon was just setting. ③ The moon rays streamed through the narrow window near my crib. 这三个分句按照时间顺序应为②③①。因而译为汉语应为：

半轮晓月渐渐西沉，月光通过小床旁边一扇窄窄的窗子射进来，我趁着月光穿上衣服。

再如：

2. He had flown in just the day before from Georgia when he had spent his vacation basking in the Caucasian sun after the completion of the construction job he had been engaged in the South.

3. It didn't take long for Manuel García Murillo, a bricklayer who took over as mayor here last June, to realize that his town was in trouble.

4. It was an old woman, tall and shapely still, though withered by time, on whom his eyes fell when he stopped and turned.

2.2 逻辑顺序

英语句子之间的逻辑顺序由连接词决定，一般开门见山，先突出句子要表达的主要信息，再叙述次要信息，而汉语句子则往往按照逻辑顺序排列，特别是在没有连接词表示句子逻辑关系时，更是如此。

2.2.1 表态与叙事

英语通常先评论或表态，然后再说明有关情况。汉语则正好相反，通常先叙事后表态。例如：

1. It is not always easy to take these solutions and replicate them in other countries, though.

然而，实施这些方案并且在其他国家如法炮制并不总是那么容易。

在上个例子中，"it"为形式主语，引导表态部分。不定式部分为真正的主语，是叙事部分。在汉译时根据汉语表达习惯先叙事，再评论或表态。再如：

2. Citizens here especially in the arts and culture community think it's fantastic that they have all these different possibilities here.

3. That could pose a threat to European markets as foreign producers like Brazil or developing countries like Indonesia and Malaysia try to ship their biofuels to markets where demand, subsidies and tax breaks are the greatest.

4. It is good that the Singapore government wants to do something about the country's preoccupation with material success. But it will be a losing battle if the family unit itself is not involved.

2.2.2 因和果

在因果关系上，英语通常直奔主题，然后再作解释。而汉语通常先原因后结果，特别是表示因果的关联词省略时更是如此。例如：

1. They had to give up the program for lack of investment funds.

因为缺乏投资资金，他们只好放弃了这项计划。

在上面的例子中，英语先叙述结果，再探讨原因，而汉语则完全相反。再如：

2. Additional social stresses may also occur because of the population explosion problems arising from mass migration movements—themselves made relatively easy nowadays by modern means of transport.

3. Though most of the contracts have many provisions in common, each is different from the others owing to the nature of the goods.

4. This week the urgency of the problem was underscored as wheat prices rose to record highs and wheat stores dropped to the lowest level in 35 years.

2.2.3 前景和背景

前景指句子中所表达的主要信息或强调的部分；背景指句子中一些如交代时间、地点、条件、原因等相对不重要的成分。英语中一般先说前景，再说背景，而汉语则往往相反。因此，在英译汉时，要理清主要脉络，以及条件、因果、时间等的逻辑关系再进行语序调整。例如：

1. Insects would make it impossible for us to live in the world; they would devour all our crops and kill our flocks and herds, if it were not for the protection we get from insect-eating animals.

上面的英语句子中包含三个短句：① Insects would make it impossible for us to live in the world; ② they would devour all our crops and kill our flocks and herds, ③ if it were not for the protection we get from insect-eating animals. 其中①句属于前景，表达句子的主要信息。②③句为背景，交代前景发生的条件。按照汉语的逻辑顺序，应为③-②-①的顺序。译文如下：

假如没有那些以昆虫为食物的动物保护我们，昆虫将吞噬我们所有的庄稼，害死我们的牛羊家畜，使我们不能生存于世。

再如：

2. Few countries rival Norway when it comes to protecting the environment and preserving indigenous customs.

3. In the developing world, the shift to more lucrative biofuel crops destined for richer countries could create serious hunger and damage the environment if wild land is converted to biofuel cultivation.

4. Similarly, private companies may calculate that it is worth bringing clean water to an area if its residents are willing to pay back the investment over many years.

练习

一、修改下列句子,注意语序调整。

1. There are many wonderful stories to tell about the places I visited and the people I met.
   原译:关于我访问的一些地方和遇见的不少人有许多奇妙的故事可以讲。
   改译:

2. For example, they do not compensate for gross social inequality, and thus do not tell how able an underprivileged youngster might have been had he grown up under more favorable circumstances.
   原译:它们无法弥补巨大的社会不公,因而也不能说明一个物质条件差的年轻人所具有的实际才能,如果他在较好的环境中成长。
   改译:

3. But just as all nations can benefit from the promise of this new world, no nation is immune to its perils. We all have a stake in building peace and prosperity, and in confronting threats that respects no borders—terrorism and drug trafficking, disease and environmental destruction.
   原译:但是,正如世界各国均会受益于这个新世界的美好前景一样,没有一个国家能够免遭其危险。我们在以下方面都有着利害关系:缔造和平与繁荣,抵御不分国界的诸多威胁——恐怖主义、贩毒、疾病和环境破坏。
   改译:

4. He found the thought infinitely more enjoyable to focus on than the niggling fear that had been troubling him since his conversation with Fisher.
   原译:他发现集中精力于这种想法无疑要比那种自从与费希尔谈话以来一直困扰着他的那种莫名其妙的担忧令人愉快得多。
   改译:

5. One day Benjamin became a practicing solipsist. Within a week his wife had run away with another man; he'd lost his job as a shipping clerk and he had broken his leg chasing a black cat to keep it from crossing his path. He decided, in his bed at the hospital, to end it all.
   原译:一天,本杰明的唯我主义观念达到了极致。在一周之内,他的妻子与另一个男人私奔,他的运输员工作也丢了,而他的腿又在一次与一只黑猫的追逐中摔断了,仅仅是为了不让这只猫从他面前经过。当他躺在医院的床上时,他决定了,决定结束这一切。

改译：

二、翻译下列句子，注意语序调整。

1. rain or shine

2. art and literature

3. enterprises of small and medium sizes

4. food, clothing, shelter and transportation

5. The job had sounded impossible when he arrived fresh off his first year of college, looking to make some summer money, still a skinny teenager with sandy blond hair and a narrow, freckled face.

6. Human history began when the inheritance of genetics and behavior which had until then provided the only way of dominating the environment was first broken through by conscious choice.

7. He is particularly doubtful that current economic progress will be able to help out the poor.

8. She was disappointed that the government had withdrawn money while continuing to support museums in London.

9. The compass needle can be used to show direction because the earth itself acts like a huge magnet.

10. Opportunities for foreign investment will expand as China undertakes economic reforms and creates financial markets.

11. People were afraid to leave their houses, for although the police had been ordered to stand by in case of emergency, they were just as confused and helpless as anybody else.

12. But those fruit and vegetables in this category that do not meet European norms will still be allowed onto the market, providing they are marked as being substandard or intended for cooking or processing.

13. A subsidy may not even be necessary, despite the agency's proposals, if a country can harness the economic benefits of providing clean water.

14. Land that was untouched could be tainted by air and water pollution as generators, smokestacks and large vehicles sprout to support the growing energy industry.

15. So when I read of how the new Remaking Singapore Committee had set one of its goals as challenging the traditional roads to success, encouraging Singaporeans to realize alternative careers in the arts, sports, research or as entrepreneurs, I had my doubts about its success in this area, if not coupled with help from parents themselves.

三、翻译下面的段落，注意语序调整。

Mrs. Clinton receives about 5,000 letters a week, according to Lawrence senior Jenny Dunlavy, who spent the fall term in D.C. as part of American University's Washington Semester Program. Working in the office of First Lady's Scheduling Correspondence, Dunlavy and other sorted through as many as 100 invitations a day requesting Mrs. Clinton to attend everything from birthday parties to baby showers.

第 11 章

分 译 法

由于英、汉两种语言表达方式的差异,不可避免地需要变换原文的句子结构和句式。英语句子繁复,修饰语多且长,句子结构复杂,一句话里常常是一个从句(或短语)套一个从句(或短语)。汉语句子简短,修饰语少且短,句子结构简单,通常呈直线型发展,层层推进。因此英译汉时往往需要化繁为简、化整为零,把英语中的某些部分,如:单词、短语或从句独立出来,分译为汉语中单独的句子,以更好地表达原文的意思,使译文更合乎汉语的表达习惯。

第 1 节 单词的分译

英语中的一些形容词或副词，看上去是修饰与其相邻的句子中的某个成分，但实际上是对整个句子所陈述的内容进行描述、评述或评价，表明说话者的观点或态度。这些形容词或副词在译为汉语时，通常需要拆分出来，译为独立的句子。例如：

1. The number of the young people in the United States who cannot read is incredible—about one in four.

在上句中，形容词"incredible"一词不是修饰其后的四分之一这个数字，而是美国青年的阅读能力差这一现象的评述，因此需分译为：

大约有四分之一的美国青年没有阅读能力，这简直令人难以置信！

再如：

2. He crashed down on a protesting chair.

3. Next door, a large-expected audience of 300 attended the Fifteenth International Conference on Laser Atmospheric Studies.

4. With the fear of largely imaginary plots against his leadership, his self-confidence seemed totally to desert him.

副词在表明说话者的观点或态度时也需单独拆分出来，例如：

5. He tried vainly to talk us into agreement with the unrealistic proposal.
他试图劝说我们同意接受这项不切实际的建议，但还是白费了力气。

上句中，副词"vainly"在语义上修饰的是整个句子，因而单独分译。再如：

6. We recognize that China's long-term modernization program understandably and necessarily emphasizes economic growth.

7. So I swam and, presumably because of the long absence of foreigners from Sichuan, before an undeservedly large and enthusiastic audience.

8. Jackson cannot politely turn down the invitation to an Arab foreign ministers conference.

第 2 节　短语的分译

英语常用短语，名词短语、介词短语、分词短语等各类短语使用广泛。这些英语短语所包含的信息或语义内涵，在汉语中往往很难找到合适的短语来表达，而需拆分译为汉语中的短句。

2.1　名词短语

名词短语在英文句子中出现频率很高，可以作句子的主语、宾语或同位语。在英译汉时，如果名词短语表达一个完整独立的意思，往往需进行分译。例如：

1. The wide gap between rich and poor in the district deserves more in-depth study and exploration.

在上句中，名词短语"the wide gap between rich and poor in the district"在句子中作主语，表达了完整的意思，即"There is a wide gap between rich and poor in the district"。因此，我们可以分译为：

这一地区贫富悬殊的情况十分严重，值得深入研究、探讨。

再如：

2. Global climate change threatens to raise sea levels by as much as four feet by the end of the century.

3. The military is forbidden to kill the vessel, a relatively easy task.

4. Brazil, a country with a perfect climate for sugar cane and vast amounts of land, started with subsidies years ago to encourage the farming of sugarcane for biofuels.

2.2　介词短语

我们前面已经分析过，英语作为静态性语言的主要标志之一是介词短语使用广泛。当介词短语含义丰富、表达完整意思时，译为汉语时往往对其进行分译。例如：

1. I found this letter very moving, with its brief portrait of an intelligent, brave man and his life of service.

我觉得这封信很感人,尽管它只简短地介绍了一个智慧、勇敢的人,及他毕生的贡献。

在上面的例子中,"with"所引导的介词短语占整个句子的三分之二左右,含有完整的信息,因而我们对其进行了分译。再如:

2. In addition, Warsaw's Chopin Museum, with the world's largest collection of Chopin documents and other artifacts, will undergo a total redesign, modernization and expansion.

3. When night falls in remote parts of Africa, hundreds of millions of people without access to electricity turn to candles or flammable kerosene lamps for illumination.

4. Once a rural community, Beaverton, population 87,000, is now the sixth largest city in Oregon—with immigration rates higher than those of Portland, Oregon's largest city.

2.3 分词短语

分词短语包括现在分词短语和过去分词短语,可在句子中作定语、状语、表语等成分,是英语不同于汉语的一种特殊语法现象。英语中的分词短语往往包含完整、复杂的意思,需分译为汉语中的短句。例如:

1. They want to sweep everything up with their dragnets and then move on, benefiting from our work and sacrifice and leaving us with nothing.

在上面的例子中包含的两个现在分词短语"benefiting from our work and sacrifice"和"leaving us with nothing"作状语表结果。这两个现在分词短语包含独立完整的意思,可分译如下:

他们想用拖网一网打尽,然后又上别处去打。我们出力,他们受益,弄得我们一无所有。

再如:

2. Coastal erosion is a problem in Alaska as well, forcing the United States to prepare to relocate several Inuit coastal villages at a projected cost of US$ 100 million or more for each one.

3. The number of children who are driven to school over all is rising in the United States and Europe, making up a sizable chunk of transportation's contribution

to greenhouse-gas emissions.

除了上面例子中的现在分词短语可分译外,英语中较长、较复杂的过去分词短语也往往需要分译。例如:

4. The plantations of Latin America are large, privately owned estates worked by tenant labor.

拉丁美洲的大庄园就是大片的私有土地,雇人劳动。

上句中,过去分词短语"worked by tenant labor"作"estates"的后置定语,因其前面已经有前置定语修饰,这一短语若再前置的话会造成定语过长,表达啰唆,因而译文对其进行了分译。再如:

5. Each year it has become harder for family farms to compete with industrial scale agriculture—heavily subsidized by the government—underselling them at every turn.

6. In India, solar power projects, often funded by micro credit institutions, are helping the country reduce carbon emissions and achieve its goal to double the contribution of renewable energy.

7. While the present century was in its teens, and on one sunshiny morning in June, there drove up to the great iron gate of Miss Pinkerton's academy for young ladies, on Chiswick Hall, a large family coach, with two fat horses in blazing harness, driven by a fat coachman in a three-concerned hat and wig, at the rate of four miles an hour.

第 3 节 句子的分译

英语有许多长句、复杂句,有许多从属、附加成分或包含定语从句、状语从句、名词性从句等的从属成分。这类句子在译为汉语时,一般需先译出主句或主干,之后把其余成分分译为一个或多个句子。例如:

1. Wheat farms are most efficient when they comprise some thousands of hectares and can be worked by teams of people and machines.

在上句中,主句为概括句,"when" 所引导的状语从句较长、较复杂,对主句进行了详细说明。我们可将其分译如下:

生产小麦的农场最有效益。它们拥有几千公顷土地,雇用一群群工人,并使用机器。

2. Among primitive people, a person is seen as a dependent part of nature, a frail reed in a harsh world governed by natural laws that must be obeyed if he is to survive.

3. It was the moment I ceased being a child, when I began to have an adult's awareness of the pain and tragedy in life.

4. The idea that the President of the United States, who had important business to take care of, would spend five minutes relaxing in laughter before the meeting was more than Stanton could endure.

5. Anyone considering taking part in a work of transformation of those forms of older art which seem to us in many ways unsatisfactory, so that they should be more in turn with the changing times, and anyone who does quail at the prospect of seeking out new forms of expression for new materials and new building functions, will find spiritual kinship, observing Borromini's buildings.

6. First, attention shifted from the individual worker to the household as a supplier of labor services; the increasing tendency of married women to enter the labor force and the wide disparities and fluctuations observed in the rate that females participate in a labor force drew attention to the fact that an individual's decision to supply labor force is not independent of the size, age structure, and asset holdings of

the household to which he or she belongs.

练习

一、翻译下列句子，注意分译法的使用。

1. He had seen the dictionary fly over the pavement of the little garden and fall at length at the feet of the astonished Mary.

2. The senior leaders' departure could curiously help the two parties sink an age-long party feud.

3. Law enforcement cannot responsibly stand aloof.

4. The strong walls of the castle served as a good defense against the attackers.

5. The immigrants—virtually all of them are men—cluster by nationality and look for work on the farms.

6. Higuera de la Serena, a cluster of about 900 houses surrounded by farmland, and traditionally dependent on pig farming and olives, got swept up in the giddy days of the construction boom.

7. Invitingly green Angel Island, once a military installation, contains meandering trails and picnic spots ideal for a day's excursion.

8. Stonehenge, once a temple with giant stone slabs aligned in a circle to mark the passage of the sun, is among the most prominent victims of the government's spending cuts.

9. With water levels falling rapidly at the peak of the dry season, a giant school of bass, a tasty fish that fetches a good price at markets, was swimming right into the nets being cast from a dozen small canoes here.

10. In Bykovsky, a village of 457 residents at the tip of a fin-shaped peninsula on Russia's northeast coast, the shoreline is collapsing, creeping closer and closer to houses and tanks of heating oil, at a rate of 15 to 18 feet, or 5 to 6 meters, a year.

11. Then they went to the southern part of the island, but found it rocky and covered with bushes, growing so thickly that it was not easy to push one's way through.

12. Motivated by generous subsidies to develop alternative energy sources, Europe's farmers are beginning to grow crops that can be turned into fuels meant to produce fewer emissions than gas or oil.

13. I leave Beijing tonight, Mr. Premier, heartened with the agreements we have reached, cheered by the frankness and fullness of our discussion.

14. It was sufficient that there was tenderness in her eyes, weakness in her manner, good nature and hope in her thoughts.

15. One of my best speeches was delivered in Hyde Park in torrents of rain to six policemen sent to watch me, plus only the secretary of the Society that had asked me to speak, who held an umbrella over me.

16. Gorbachev's letter apparently was in reply to one Reagon wrote several weeks ago urging Soviet leader to consider holding a second superpower summit this fall.

17. My opinion of you is that no man knows better than you when to speak and when others to speak for you; when to make scenes and threaten resignation; and when to be as cool as a cucumber.

18. Young men who have some reason to fear that they will be killed in battle may justifiably feel bitter in the thought that they have been cheated of the best things that life has to offer.

19. All this had come to an end in 1905 when the medical mission was dissolved and several of Mother's colleagues were killed in the uprising.

20. I am usually skeptical about any research that concludes that people are either happier or unhappier or more or less certain of themselves than they were 50 years ago.

二、翻译下面的段落,注意分译法的使用。

Alternately comforting and threatening, the realization of China's entrance into the modern world increasing qualifies the sensibility of Anglo-European nations. The thought is comforting to those who feel that the engagements made possible by virtue of a common ground are far more productive than the infrequent and one-sided contacts that, until recently perhaps, have done little to help and much to harm the Chinese people. And China's entrance into the family of nations is threatening to those who recognize the vast potentialities for economic and military growth possessed by an awakening China, and who, as well, sense that China's "enlightenment" may come at the expense of the West.

第 12 章

合 译 法

　　分译与合译是两种相辅相成的翻译技巧。一般说来，英语的句子要比汉语长，比汉语句子结构复杂，因此英译汉时分译法使用较多。但是英文中一些较短、较简单的句子，特别是口语化的句子，由于它们之间联系紧密或有重复部分，我们做英译汉时应把它们合并起来，以达到更好的效果。

第 1 节　单词的合译

英语句子中有时会用同义词或近义词表达一个意思,以达到强调的效果。汉译时,如将其全部直接译过来,往往会造成表达上的啰唆,所以,一般使用合译法只翻译一个词的含义或取两个词含义的综合。例如:

1. We must reach our goals and aims.

我们必须达到目的。

在上面的例子中,"goals"和"aims"是同义词,翻译时被合译为"目的"。再如:

2. You will supply financial power, and we'll supply man power. Isn't that fair and square?

3. His father is a man who forgives and forgets.

4. I hate all these hustles and bustles.

第 2 节　句子的合译

和单词的合译相比，句子的合译比较复杂。无论是简单句和简单句之间，还是复合句和复合句之间，或者简单句和复合句之间，甚至复合句的主句和从句之间，它们都可以合并。

2.1　简单句的合译

英译汉时简单句和简单句之间的合译一般包含两种情形。首先，在英语中，有时两个或两个以上简单句之间存在着逻辑上的相互关联，在翻译时，我们常常以其中表达主要信息的简单句为基础，把其他的简单句合并为它的某一个成分，如状语、定语、同位语等。例如：

1. It was half past ten. Mary watched the path anxiously.

十点半钟的时候，玛丽焦急地朝着小路张望。

在上面的例子中，第一句交代了后面整个故事发生的时间，所以在英语中单独表达。但在译为汉语时，根据汉语表达习惯，我们将它译为了第二句的状语。

2. His father had a small business in the city of Pisa. This city is in the north of Italy near the sea.

3. He has been ill for many years. He died in loneliness finally.

4. The river is very wide. One cannot see the opposite bank.

5. He came back to his hometown. He has left it for quite many years.

其次，当两个或两个以上的英语简单句有相同或相关的主语时，由于汉语一般不重复主语，也不喜欢用代词作主语，所以在译为汉语时把第二次出现的主语省译，把几个简单句合译为汉语中的复合句。另外，当简单句之间存在一定的逻辑关系时，也可以合译，但有时需增加必要的连接词，以表明主从之间的关系，有时需进行适当的语序调整。例如：

6. Pitcher was a quiet man. He didn't usually let his face show his feelings.

皮切尔不爱说话，也不轻易在脸上显露喜怒哀乐。

在上面的例子中，前后两句的主语都指的是"Pitcher"，所以第二句中的主语"he"被省译，与第一句合并成了汉语中的复合句。再如：

7. She is very busy at home. She had to take care of children and do the kitchen work.

8. The young man was very miserable. He had no money about him. All his savings had been stolen.

9. He was shocked. Never before had anyone come alone, on foot, to his father's cabin.

2.2 简单句与复合句的合译

同简单句与简单句合译成复合句相似，当简单句和复合句之间共享相同或相关的主语，或者存在逻辑关联时，也可以合译。例如：

1. I felt approaching footsteps. I stretched out my hand as I supposed to my mother.

我感到有人走近，便伸出了手，以为是把手伸向母亲。

这句出自海伦·凯勒的《假如给我三天光明》，描述的是她第一次见到莎莉文老师的情景。因为前后两句主语一致，所以可以合并。再如：

2. Confucius was a believer in moral action and in what we today call human development. He advocated the establishment of harmony within the social order.

3. Poets as we know have always made a great use of alliteration. They are persuaded that the repetition of a sound gives an effect of beauty.

4. Although the size of the task waiting to be carried out is daunting and there are many hurdles to be overcome, it would be wrong to end my address on a note of pessimism. Many countries have already made considerable progress in this regard.

5. The real reason why prices were, and still are, too high is complicated. No short discussion can satisfactorily explain this problem.

2.3　复合句的合译

复合句的合译包含两种情形。首先，一些英语中的复合句，可以省译连接词，把主句和从句进行压缩，译为汉语中的简单句，使表达更加凝练。例如：

1. The diagnosis seems in every case to correspond exactly with all the sensations that I have ever felt.

每次看病的诊断似乎都和我所有的感觉完全相符。

在上面的例子中，英语带有定语从句的复合句被合并成了汉语中的简单句。再如：

2. Today, there are still thousands of places which are inaccessible to tourists.

3. From Florence the river Arno ran down to Pisa, and then it reached the sea.

4. When we praise the Chinese leadership and the people, we are not merely being polite.

其次，复合句在相互关联时，我们也可以对其进行合译。例如：

5. We should try to catch up with those who are ahead of us. We should help those who are behind us.

我们不仅要赶先进，还要帮后进。

在上例中，两个复合句的主语都是"we"，所以具备合并基础。再如：

6. If you address the enquiries to an individual, your letter may have to wait while he is away. Or you make a mistake and address it to the wrong individual, and this will also mean delay.

7. A man in a newish suburb feels that he has one foot in the city and one in the country. As this is the kind of compromise he likes, he is happy.

练习

一、翻译下列句子，注意合译法的使用。

1. The room is cozy and comfortable.

2. Her son was wise and clever, but her daughter was silly and foolish.

3. He would miss many things and many people. He would miss Celia.

4. Sam had vanished. A morning came. And he was missing from work.

5. It was 2 a.m. on a hot August night. In a San Francisco suburb, a man staggered out of a bar.

6. He was very clean. His mind was open.

7. This novel is of no great literary merit. It is merely a pot-boiler.

8. I wasn't an enemy. In fact or in feeling, I was an ally.

9. I was slow to understand the deep grievance of women. This was because, as a boy, I had envied them.

10. As the year approaches its end, our tech support from vendors will be very slim. They are all busy filling early orders. This is another reason to close the shop for now.

11. I never saw anyone wear an expression of such deep gloom. He was staring into space. He looked as though the burdens of the whole world sat on his shoulders.

12. The Post Office was helpful, and Marconi applied in June, 1896, for the world's first radio patent.

13. Her dress was grey and plain, but it fitted her body nicely.

14. The distribution (of labor force employed in agriculture) in the early 1980s ranged from 67 percent of those employed in Africa to less than 5 percent in North America. In Western Europe, the figure was about 16 percent; in Eastern Europe and the Soviet Union, about 32 percent; and in Asia, about 68 percent.

15. It knows, for example, that the risk of a man being killed in a plane accident is less than the risk he takes in crossing a busy road. This enables it to quote low figures for travel insurance.

二、翻译下面的段落，注意合译法的使用。

I find it hard to believe how many people now get divorced, how many submit to such extraordinary pain. There are no clean divorces. Divorces should be conducted in abattoirs or surgical wards. In my own case, I think it would have been easier if my ex-wife had died. I would have been gallant at her funeral and shed real tears—far easier than string across a table, telling each other it was over.

It was a killing thing to look at the mother of my children and know that we would not be together for the rest of our lives. It was terrifying to say good-bye, to reject part of my own history.

How does it happen that two people who once loved each other, who felt incomplete in the absence of the other, are brought to that moment of grisly illumination when they decide it has gone irretrievably wrong? How can love change its garments and come disguised as indifference, anger, even loathing?

第 13 章

被动句的翻译

　　被动句在英语和汉语中都是重要的句式。从使用频度上来看，英语中被动结构使用较为频繁，尤其是在科技文体或新闻文体中，为了强调客观性和准确性而大量使用被动语态。在古汉语中被动语态曾被称为"不幸语态"，表达对主语而言不如意或不企望的事。虽然受以英语为代表的其他语言的影响，汉语中被动句的使用范围有所扩大，贬义色彩也逐渐削弱，但相比较而言汉语中被动语态的使用仍远不及英语频繁。

　　语言是信息的载体。一般来说，英语和汉语中的每个句子都既可以用主动语态又可以用被动语态来表达其所传递的信息。主动句和其相应的被动句作为对客观现象、过程、行为或事实的反映，在语义上是相同的。但对于同一语义，主动语态和被动语态强调的侧重点往往不同，也就是说，其所传递的信息焦点往往不同。

　　基于布拉格派提出的信息结构论，英语被动句焦点之争由来已久，主要分为强调受事者说和强调实施者说两大类。强调受事者说的语言学家认为句子的主语一般为人们关注的中心，因此被动句中动作的受事者，即主语，为所传递信息的焦点，认为若要强调动作的受事者，选择被动语态较为适宜。

　　在 20 世纪 60 年代，许多西方学者开始质疑被动句焦点为受事者这一观点。其中，俄罗斯语言学家巴赫金最先指出被动句中句子的焦点为处于句尾的施事者。我国著名语法学家章振邦在其1999年再版的《新编英语语法教程》中持相同观点。钟书能教授在其于1997年发表在《外语界》上的文章里同样指出："根据系统功能语法理论及大量语言事实，我们认为被动句中（主位）主语不是被强调的成分，相反，位于述位部分的成分才是信息核心所在，即为强调的成分。"

综上所述，主动句与被动句的差异主要在于语用功能上的不同。一个主动语态的句子和一个被动语态的句子，在信息结构上是完全不同的。在被动句的英译汉过程中，我们应根据强调信息的不同，选用不同的处理方法，以把握好原文信息焦点的翻译，真正做到被动句翻译在语义和语言的交际功能两个方面的对等。

一般情况下，英语被动句可分为带施动者的被动句和不带施动者的被动句两种。我们将主要从这两方面研究英译汉时被动句的翻译。

第1节　带施动者的被动句

带施动者的被动句在英语被动句中比例较小，只占 20% 左右。在英语被动句中需要指明施动者的情况主要有两种：一种是施动者在前文没有出现过，为新信息；另一种是施动者较长，放在句尾以避免头重脚轻。在这两种情况下，施动者的位置都需保留在句尾，以示强调。我们在翻译时可以把其译为汉语中有标志的被动句或判断句。

1.1　译为有标志的被动句

带施动者的被动句一般译为汉语有标志的被动句。但需要注意，汉语的被动标记较为繁杂，除了最常见的"被"之外，还可以用"受""遭""所""获""给""由""把""使""加以""予以""蒙"等，我们应在不同的语境下选择适当的词语。例如：

1. The plan is going to be examined first by the research group.

原译：研究小组将首先研究一下这个计划。

改译：计划将先由研究小组加以研究。

比较上面两种译文，第一种关心的是研究小组将干什么，而第二种关心的是这个计划将"遭受"什么。显然，第二种译文与原句强调一致，都是研究小组这一动作的施动者。因而，我们在翻译时保留被动形式，以在语用功能上使英汉两句强调的中心保持一致。再如：

2. Every business can be seriously affected by government laws or regulations.

3. The surface of a metal is attacked by various gases in the atmosphere.

4. Last year the region was visited by the worst drought in 100 years.

5. This new theory has now been adopted by many scientists who are searching for life in outer space.

6. Washington D. C. has always been sheltered by the federal government.

1.2　译为判断句

汉语中常用判断句"……是……的"这一句式来说明人和事物的客观情

况。这种结构在语义上往往具有被动的含义,与英语中的被动结构所表达的语义相似。例如:

1. The sign language is used by the deaf people.

这种手势语是聋哑人使用的语言。

在上面的译文中,判断句强调了"聋哑人使用的",即英文原句中的述位部分,其语用功能与原句一致。再如:

2. The telephone is invented by Alexander Graham Bell in 1876.

3. Culture is produced by creative and innovative individuals, groups and organizations.

4. The Verrazano bridge, which was designed by Othmar Ammann, joins Brooklyn to Staten Island.

1.3 译为主动句

有时,根据上下文的需要,英语中有施动者的被动句也可译为汉语主动句,而强调信息仍保持不变。例如:

1. He hadn't seen my family before, and was greatly taken with the beauty of Sophia and the little boy.

他以前从来没有见过我的家人,索菲亚和小男孩的美貌深深吸引了他。

在上面的例子中,并列复合句中的第二句译为了主动句,以和第一句进行衔接。再如:

2. Galileo, among others, recognized the problem, but failed to solve it. The problem was then attacked by Torricelli.

第 2 节　不带施动者的被动句

在英语中，无施动者的被动句的出现频率远远大于有施动者的被动句。施动者之所以不出现，一般是因为施动者一目了然或根本不知道谁是施动者。在这种情况下，动作行为的接受者往往是前面提到的已知信息，被动结构是用来强调突出动作或行为的本身或其结果。在这种情况下，英语被动句在汉译时一般不用改变被动语态，应译为汉语中相应的被动句。

2.1　译为有标志的被动句

英语不带施动者的被动句常可以译为汉语有标志的被动句。例如：

1. But all these problems were finally solved.

但是这些问题最终被解决了。

上面的例子是一个典型的英语无施动者的被动句译为汉语有被动词的被动句的情况。再如：

2. If the DNA is destroyed, the cell can not divide, and will die.

3. Until recently, scientists knew little about life in the deep sea, nor had they reason to believe that it was being threatened.

2.2　译为判断句

当英语不带施动者的被动句后有时间、地点等状语时，也可以译为汉语中的判断句。例如：

1. Voltage is not checked with this meter.

电压不是用这块仪表检查的。

在上句中，判断句强调了"用这块仪表检查的"，与英语原句强调的内容一致。再如：

2. Printing was introduced into Europe from China.

3. The AIDS virus was found in human white blood cells in 1983.

2.3　译为无标志的被动句

在汉语中，有些句子在形式上是主动的，即没有"被"等被动词的标志，但在意义上是被动的。在现代汉语中，不采用"被"字的被动句比使用"被"字等被动词的被动句要多得多。例如：

1. In the absence of a settlement through negotiation, the case under dispute can be submitted to arbitration.

如果谈判得不到解决，争执之事可提交仲裁机构。

上面这个例子把英文被动句译为了汉语无标志的被动句，即形式上看是主动的句子。如果硬要译出"被"字等汉语中被动句标志词，反而生硬了。再如：

2. Many of the world's coral species are found at depths of more than 200 meters.

3. Now these scattershot efforts are being urgently consolidated and systematized.

4. The findings have been published in the journal *Nature*.

5. In addition, the chemicals used in construction and the percentage of waste materials have been kept to a minimum, as required by both Danish and Swedish laws.

2.4 译为主动句

英语被动句中的主语之前为不定冠词"a, an"或没有冠词（零冠词）时，英语被动句中的主语通常表达的是需要强调的新信息。但是汉语被动句的主语却没有这种语用功能。因此，这类英语被动句译为汉语时，需调整语序，可译为汉语中"人们，我们，大家"等作主语的泛指主语句。例如：

1. Cement is known to be a very useful building material.

大家都知道水泥是很有用的建筑材料。

在上个例子中，汉语增加大家这个泛指主语作主语，那么句子强调的信息在水泥这一宾语上，与英文原句强调的信息一致。再如：

2. Copper articles have been used for several thousand years.

3. Vast new deposits of minerals and gems are being discovered as Greenland's massive ice cap recedes, forming the basis of a potentially lucrative mining industry.

当英语被动句中的主语表达需要强调的新信息时，还可以译为汉语中的无主语句。这种句式在汉语中很常见，而英文中一般只存在于祈使句中。一般情况下，如果英语被动句中主语是新信息，且表达态度、告诫、要求，那么可将其译为汉语的无主语句。例如：

4. Stipulated under Clause 12 of this contract, payment shall be effected within 10 days after receipt of the shipping documents.

根据本合同第 12 款约定，必须在接到装运单据以后的 10 天内付款。

上个例子中的英语句子被译为了汉语中的无主语句，译文强调的是"付款"，与英语原文强调的信息一致。再如：

5. To get all the stages of the ground, a first big push is needed.

6. Visitors are requested to leave their coats in the cloak-room.

7. Clearly something else has to be done in order to avoid an eventual ecological disaster.

8. Smokers must be warned that doctors have reached the conclusion that smoking increases the possibility of lung cancer.

9. If steps are taken quickly to prevent this kind of destructive activity from occurring on the high seas, the benefits both to the marine environment and to future generations are incalculable.

有时英语被动句中没有出现"by"引导的施动者，而代之以一个状语。这个状语一般由介词短语表达，其在多数情况下表示地点、目的和方式。此时可以把主语译成宾语，把状语移到主语位置。例如：

10. Commercial farming, or production for cash, is usually done on large farms.

大农场通常从事商业耕种，或者说为赚钱而生产。

在上例中，英文"on large farms"本在句尾，译为汉语时却被调整到了句首，符合汉语表达习惯。再如：

11. Laws to deter people from texting at the wheel have been implemented across the globe.

12. Pre-school education may also be provided in some private day nurseries and pre-school playgroups (which are largely organized by parents).

此外,以 it 作为形式主语的英语被动句,也常译成主动形式,有时不加主语,有时则加上泛指主语。例如:

13. It is generally accepted that the experiences of the child in his first years largely determine his character and later personality.

人们普遍认为,孩子们的早年经历在很大程度上决定了他们的性格及其未来的人品。

在上例中,我们增加了泛指主语"人们"来翻译"it"作为形式主语的英语被动句,以进行表态。再如:

14. It is said that the production of transistor radios was increased six times from 1970 to 1974.

15. It has been calculated that only 1/10,000 part of the energy radiated annually from the sun is taken up by plants.

练习

一、翻译下列英语被动句。

1. The design will be examined by a special committee.

2. Sometimes the communication would be seriously disturbed by solar spots.

3. Each of the body systems is regulated in some way by some part of the endocrine system.

4. America was discovered by Columbus in 1492.

5. And the astonishing thing is that this most dangerous operation was organized by a young attractive twenty-three-year old Belgian girl, Andree De Jongh by name.

6. The words "work" and "power" are often confused or interchanged in colloquial use.

7. The American trade delegation was given a hearty welcome.

8. Agricultural income is also derived from non-food crops such as rubber, fiber plants, tobacco, and oilseeds used in synthetic chemical compounds.

9. Even some money from the European Union that was supposed to be used for routine operating expenses and last until 2013 has already been spent.

10. In granting Greenland home rule in 2009, Denmark froze its annual subsidy, which is scheduled to be decreased further in the coming years.

11. The speed of the molecules is increased when they are heated.

12. Mrs. Norris, having asked one or two questions about the dinner, which were not immediately attended to, seemed almost determined to say no more.

13. Steel can be made so hard that it will cut iron.

14. Since 2010, more than 150 coal plants have been closed or scheduled for retirement.

15. No major improvements have been made to the facilities there since they were built 40 years ago.

16. Attention must be paid to safety in handling radioactive materials.

17. In the meantime, some local solutions are being found.

18. Great efforts should be made to inform young people especially of the dreadful consequences of taking up the habit.

19. Actually, Chopin doesn't need to be promoted, but we hope that Poland and Polish culture can be promoted through Chopin.

20. It is estimated that roughly half of the world's highest seamounts—areas that rise from the ocean floor and are particularly rich in marine life—are also found in the deep ocean.

二、翻译下面的段落，注意被动句的翻译。

As oil is found deep in the ground, its presence cannot be determined by a study of the surface. Consequently, a geological survey of the underground rocks structure must be carried out. If it is thought that the rocks in a certain area contain oil, a "drilling rig" is assembled. The most obvious part of a drilling rig is called "a derrick." It is used to lift sections of pipe, which are lowered into the hole made by the drill. As the hole is being drilled, a steel pipe is pushed down to prevent the sides from falling in. If oil is struck, a cover is firmly fixed to the top of the pipe and the oil is allowed to escape through a series of valves.

第14章

定语从句

　　定语从句是英语中使用得最频繁的从句之一，也是给英语句子理解带来严重干扰的因素之一。英语定语从句为右开放型，从理论上讲，它可以向右扩展成无数个从句。而汉语中只有定语修饰语而没有定语从句，汉语中的定语成分通常放在所修饰词的前面，即左边，定语不能过多或过长，不能任意扩展。在翻译定语从句时，我们不能只从语法关系上去把握定语从句，还要从语用功能上去把握它。定语从句不能被简单地译为"……的"这种前置字结构，其翻译方法是灵活多样的。总的来说，无论是限制性定语从句的翻译，还是非限制性定语从句的翻译，一般都可采用合译法、分译法和转译法。

第 1 节 合 译 法

一般来说,当定语从句,特别是限制性定语从句,句子较短、较简单,用于表示一个事物,具有"区别"、"分类"和"限定"等语用功能时,在翻译时采用合译法,即把定语从句这种主从复合句译成汉语中的简单句,以避免不必要的重复,使句子简单明了、语义清晰、逻辑严密。使用合译法时,有时需把从句译成词组,或将某些重复部分省略。

1.1 前置法

许多具有"区别"、"分类"和"限定"等语用功能的定语从句在译为汉语时被直接译到所修饰词的前面作定语,从而将英语复合句译成汉语简单句。这也是定语从句最常见的翻译方法。例如:

1. None of the ones we investigated really would produce the results that would meet the requirements.

我们试用的方法确实都不能产生达标的结果。

在上面的例子中,两个较短的、表示限定的定语从句"we investigated"和"that would meet the requirements"都译为了前置定语,以限定先行词的语义。再如:

2. The 4 million Russian people who live north of the Arctic Circle are feeling the effects of warming in many ways.

3. Education is the most powerful weapon we have to address that problem.

4. Her laugh, which was very infectious, broke the silence.

5. The activities, goods and services they create, produce and distribute have a value which is cultural, social and economic.

6. The teachers may be too busy with kids who misbehave and see out the child who stays in the shadows, however.

1.2 融合法

在含有定语从句的复合句中,当主句仅起结构上的作用时,本身的语义并不突出，而定语从句反而在意义上突出了全句的重点，在译为汉语时采用融合法，把定语从句译为谓语，或者兼语式或连动式的一部分。例如：

1. There have been good results in the experiment that have given him great encouragement.

实验中的良好结果给了他莫大的鼓舞。

在上面的例子中，主句为"there be"句型，并未表达主要语义。句子的主要语义体现在定语从句中，因而，定语从句译为了谓语。再如：

2. We have a social and political system which differs in many respects from your own.

3. His phone rings regularly from other town officials who want to know how to do the same thing.

兼语式是汉语中的一种特殊句式。当定语从句中的先行词在定语从句中充当主语或宾语，即先行词在逻辑上与定语从句中的动词构成主谓或动宾关系时，有时可以把英语中含有此类定语从句的主从复合句译为汉语中的兼语式，以使译文更加简洁、紧凑。例如：

4. I need someone who can instruct me in my English study.

我需要一个人来指导我学习英语。

在上面的例子中，我们省译了"who"，把英语定语从句译为了汉语典型的兼语式句子。再如：

5. When I passed by, I saw a man who was quarreling with his wife.

6. Despite the new tunnel, there are still a few people who rashly attempt to cross the pass on foot.

7. That is due in part to the presence of the BBC, Britain's state-controlled main broadcaster which has no advertising.

此外，为了行文方便，当定语从句中的主句、从句中的动词是相继发生时，可以在英译汉时把主句和从句中的动词连起来一起翻译，译为汉语中的连动式，这样可以使句子更加连贯，符合汉语的表达习惯。例如：

8. We will send the boy to Britain, where he can receive better education.

我们要把这个孩子送到英国，接受更好的教育。

在上面的例子中,主句中的"送到英国"和定语从句中的"接受更好的教育"是相继发生的,因而被译为汉语中的连动式。再如:

9. He took out a bottle of wine out of his pocket, which he began to drink slowly.

10. As she turned the corner a new idea occurred to her, which made her stop dead.

第 2 节 分 译 法

当非限制性定语从句或较长的限制性定语从句的语用功能为描述功能，与主句形成描述关系，表达一个事件时，定语从句的翻译一般采用分译法。根据时间顺序和逻辑重点译作汉语联合复句中前置或后置的分句，或译作独立的句子。一般而言，在翻译中可重述先行词或省译先行词。例如：

1. They are chasing their counterparts in the Americas who have been raising crops for biofuel for more than five years.

他们正在追随美国同伴，后者种植用于生物燃料的作物已超过 5 年。

在上面的例子中，先行词 "their counterparts in the Americas" 是名词性词组，语义具体、确切、完整，而限制性定语从句叙述事件，因而译为汉语时对其进行了分译，重述了先行词，将定语从句单独译为了一个句子。再如：

2. Tucked away in this small village in Buckinghamshire County is the former Elizabethan coaching inn where William Shakespeare is said to have penned part of *A Midsummer Night's Dream*.

3. Google's Assistant, which began in its Pixel phone but has moved to other Android devices, speaks four languages.

4. The report attributed the persistent income gap in Washington to the area's special job opportunities, which attract high-income households.

有时，定语从句中的关系代词或关系副词在译为汉语时也可省略不译，与主句连贯叙述。例如：

5. NASA is hiring someone who can defend Earth from alien contamination.

美国国家航天局（NASA）正在招募新成员以负责保护地球免受外来入侵。

在上面的例子中，因为主句中的宾语即为定语从句中关系代词 "who" 所指代的部分，所以汉译时对其进行了省译，以避免重复。再如：

6. Settled by immigrants from northern Europe in the 19th century, today it is

a place where 80 languages from Albanian to Urdu are spoken in the public schools and about 30 percent of students speak a language besides English.

7. The crew on board was just waiting for the remainder of the fish to move into the river's main channel, where they intended to scoop up as many as they could with their efficient gill nets.

8. He served throughout the war as a general surgeon with an airborne special forces unit in Europe, where he became one of the war's most highly decorated physicians.

有时，在非限制性定语从句中，关系代词并不是指代先行词，而是指代整个主句或部分主句的内容。这时，定语从句可译为"这……"，用以对主句进行复指。例如：

9. We took a short cut through the woods, which saved about twenty minutes.
我们抄近路穿过树林，这样我们少花了大约 20 分钟。

在上面的例子中，非限制性定语从句中"which"指代的是前面的整个主句，因而用"这样"对主句的意思进行替代，被单独分译成句。再如：

10. The relations between China and the United States of America have been improved, which will contribute to our four modernizations and world peace.

11. Anta is also sponsoring the China Basketball Association, for the second year running, which will raise its profile.

此外，定语从句在分译时，有时需按时间和逻辑顺序重新调整语序，把定语从句译为前置分句，例如：

12. She suddenly thought of her husband, who had left her and their children behind and had never been heard of.
她丈夫早就抛弃了妻儿一直杳无音信，现在她突然想起了他。

在上面的例子中，定语从句叙述的事情发生在主句之前，因而在汉译时，按照时间顺序对其进行了语序调整。再如：

13. They remarked now he took a different seat from that which he usually occupied when he chose to attend divine worship.

14. It leads visitors to dozens of sites in Warsaw and elsewhere around the country where the composer lived, ate, studied, performed, visited or even partied.

15. Josette Sheeran, the new head of the United Nations World Food Program, which fed nearly 90 million people in 2006, said that biofuels created new problems.

第3节 转 译 法

英语中有些定语从句在表层结构上虽为定语，但实际上却起状语的作用，此时可将其转译成汉语中的偏正复句，以表达原因、结果、目的、假设、条件、让步或转折等关系，或将其转译为时间状语短语，以说明主句所描述事件发生的时间。例如：

1. Electronic computers, which have many advantages, cannot carry out creative work and replace man.

虽然电子计算机有很多优点，但它不能进行创造性工作，也代替不了人。

上面例子中的定语从句含有让步意义，将其译为汉语让步状语从句，可以使语句更连贯、意思更清楚。再如：

2. This denial, which is contrary to the letter and spirit of the law, is being appealed.

3. But officials at the European Commission say they are pursuing a measured course that will prevent some of the price and supply problems seen in American markets.

4. Emergency measures must be taken to eliminate the air pollution of a city, which, as reported by the control center, exceeds tolerance limit and endangers the safety of the inhabitants.

5. I once met with Dr. Li in the street, who came back to see his parents in 1995.

6. A driver who is driving the bus mustn't talk with others or be absent-minded.

练习

一、翻译下列句子，注意其中定语从句的翻译。

1. He is on a path typical for someone who attended college without getting a four-year degree.

2. Apple may well be the only technical company on the planet that would dare compare itself to Picasso.

3. Ivana Trump, the first wife of President Donald Trump, is writing a memoir that will focus on the couple's three children.

4. A pessimist is one who makes difficulties of his opportunities; an optimist is one who makes opportunities of his difficulties.

5. The conditions that determine what will be raised in an area include climate, water supply, and terrain.

6. It was one of those days that the peasant fishermen on this tributary of the Amazon River dream about.

7. He had great success in football which made him an idol in the eyes of every football player.

8. The serviceman will send the washing machine to the repair shop, where it will be checked and repaired.

9. It was a Shanghai scholar who was then traveling in London who came up with the perfect translation "Ke Kou Ke Le" for Coca-Cola in a name search competition in the 1930s. The Chinese characters, which means "delicious and happy," were an instant hit, and it has become one of the most popular brand names in Chinese ever since.

10. One was a violent thunderstorm, the worst I had ever seen, which obscured my objective.

11. The school system of reaching for A's underlies the country's culture, which emphasizes the chase for economic excellence where wealth and status are must-haves.

12. The strange fact about radiation is that it can harm without causing pain, which

is the warning signal we expect from injuries.

13. But we are much less conscious of the extent to which work provides the cultural life that can make the difference between a full or an empty life.

14. This will be epoch-making revolution in China's social productive forces which will lay down the material foundation for the socialist and communist mode of production.

15. He runs a firm of handymen which helps with everything from fixing curtain rods to stopping a dripping tap. His employees mainly come from the generation of 50-somethings who have a lifetime of handyman experience doing stuff for friends and family.

16. This sum is in addition to the nearly US＄1 billion that DHL has already invested in the Greater China region, which accounts for over half of its more than US＄1.7 billion investment in Asia Pacific from 2001 to 2006.

17. Power is equal to work divided by the time, as has been said before.

18. Advertisers also like the efficiency of the medium: much of the advertising on the net is "pay-per-click," which means that advertisers pay only when consumers click on an ad, so they can be relatively confident that their advertisements are reaching a receptive audience.

19. Scientists believed that there must be hundreds of heavenly bodies in the universe where human beings or something like human beings may exist.

20. The men suddenly awakened to the fact that there were beauty and significance in these trifles, which they had so long trodden carelessly beneath their feet.

21. He wanted changes, and those changes would not benefit the rich to whose school he had gone and to whose circles he had moved.

22. The U.S. maintains enormous armies and gigantic navies which are used not merely for its defense.

23. Electrical energy that is supplied to the motor may be converted into mechanical energy of motion.

24. In the Third World, where two out of three people still live by farming, food shortage and malnutrition are common.

25. To succeed in this area, one needs profound knowledge and experience, which few has.

26. A new product, which has beautiful packing, good quality and advertising, may very likely be a hit in markets.

27. As stocks of the most popular species diminish to worrisome levels, tensions are growing between subsistence fishermen and their commercial rivals, who are eager to enrich their bottom line and satisfy the growing appetite for fish of city-dwellers in Brazil and abroad.

28. Similar research has previously showed smartphones can have a "butterfly brain effect" on users that can cause mental blunders.

29. Under a compromise reached with national governments, many of which opposed the changes, standards will remain for 10 types of fruit and vegetables, including apples, peaches, pears, strawberries and tomatoes.

30. The child must protect himself from an educator who masters his thoughts and inclination or rudely handles, who without consideration betrays or makes ridiculous most sacred feelings, who exposes faults or praises characteristics before strangers, or even uses an open-hearted, confidential confession as an occasion for reproof at another time.

二、翻译下面的段落,注意其中定语从句的翻译。

I, by comparison, living in my overpriced city apartment, walking to work past putrid sacks of street garbage, paying usurious taxes to local and state governments I generally abhor, am rated middle class. This causes me to wonder, do the measurement make sense? Are we measuring only that which easily measured—the numbers on the money chart—and ignoring values more central to the good life?

For my sons there is of course the rural bounty of fresh-grown vegetables, line-caught fish and the shared riches of neighbors' orchards and gardens. There is the unpaid baby-sitter for whose children my daughter-in-law baby-sits in return, and neighbours who barter their skills and labour. But more than that, how do you measure serenity? Sense of self?

I don't want to idealize life in small places. There are times when the outside world intrudes brutally, as when the cost of gasoline goes up or developers cast their eyes on untouched farmland; there are cruelties, there is intolerance, and there are all the many vices and meannesses in small places that exist in large cities. Furthermore, it is harder to ignore them when they cannot be banished psychologically to another part of town or excused as the whims of alien groups—when they have to be acknowledged as "part of us."

第 15 章

状语从句

　　英语状语从句包括表示时间、地点、条件、目的、让步、因果等关系的各种从句。这些从句一般与主句之间为从属关系。与定语从句的翻译相比，英语状语从句的翻译要相对简单、容易，因为引导英语状语从句的连词大多能在汉语中找到相应的关联词进行翻译。但是，英语状语从句的位置远比定语从句灵活得多，种类也更加多样，所以我们在把英语状语从句译为汉语时需要首先厘清主句和从句之间的关系，然后再根据时间、空间、逻辑、心理等顺序对状语从句进行语序调整，同时结合分译、合译、转译等翻译方法和技巧，将其译为汉语中恰当的句式。

第 1 节 时间状语从句

1.1 译为汉语中相应的时间状语

英语中的时间状语从句一般可译为汉语中相应的时间状语，但是因为英语中时间状语从句的位置比较灵活，可放在句首或句尾，而汉语中的时间状语多位于句首，所以在翻译时需要根据情况调整语序。例如：

1. When the light waves strike the earth, part of their energy changes back to heat again.

当光波照射到地球上时，其部分能量又转变为热能。

在上面的例子中，英语中的"when"引导的时间状语从句位于句首，同汉语表达习惯一致，所以不需调整。再如：

2. When they approached Trenton, lights were still burning in many of the houses and Christmas parties were still going on.

3. We shall discuss the problem fully before we make the decision.

4. Art museums have watched this development nervously, fearing damage to their collections or to visitors, as users swing their sticks with abandon.

1.2 译为汉语中并列复合句

英语中的一些时间状语从句中的连词在译为汉语时可以省译，把时间状语从句和主句译为汉语中的并列复合句，以使译文流畅，符合汉语表达习惯。在省译连词时，需根据时间顺序或逻辑顺序进行语序调整。

1. She sang as she prepared the experiment.

她一边唱歌，一边准备实验。

在上面的例子中，我们将英语的主从复合句译为了汉语的并列句。再如：

2. The earth turns round its axis as it travels about the sun.

3. They set him free when his ransom had not yet been paid.

1.3 译为汉语中的主句

有时，英语时间状语从句中的"when"相当于"just at that time when"或"suddenly（all of a sudden）"之意。在这种情况下，句子的语义重心在从句上，因而需把英语时间状语从句译为汉语的主句。例如：

1. My friend and I had just finished lunch at an expensive restaurant when we realized that we didn't have enough money to pay the bill.

我和我朋友在一家豪华餐馆刚刚用完午餐，突然意识到我们带的钱不够付账。

在上面的例子中，"when"所引导的时间状语从句表示用餐时突然发生的状况，所以被转译为了主句。再如：

2. A young boy and his grandmother were walking along the shore in Miami Beach when a huge wave appeared out of nowhere, sweeping the child out to sea.

3. I was just about to make my little bow of assent, when the meaning of these last words sank in, jolting me out of my sad reverie.

1.4 译为汉语其他状语从句

有些英语状语从句虽然在形式上是由表示时间的引导词（如 when, before, until 等）引导，但根据句子逻辑意义来判断，它应被灵活翻译成汉语中表示因果、条件、转折或目的等关系的状语从句。例如：

1. Why do it when you stand only to lose by it?

既然干这事只会让你吃亏，你为什么还要干呢？

在上面的例子中，"when"所引导的时间状语从句在语义上与主句之间是让步关系，因而被译为了汉语中的让步状语从句。再如：

2. When you sit with a nice girl for 2 hours, you think it's only a minute, but when you sit on a hot stove for a minute, you think it's two hours. That's relativity.

3. She had chosen to stay among poor folks when she might have had everything of the best.

4. Before manned spacecraft could be sent to space, the problem of getting the spacecraft safely back to the earth had to be solved.

第 2 节　地点状语从句

2.1　译为汉语中相应的地点状语

英语中的地点状语从句一般可译为汉语中的地点状语。同时间状语从句一样，英语中地点状语从句的位置也很灵活，可位于主句之前，也可置于主句之后，而汉语地点状语通常位于主句之前，因而翻译时也需要视情况进行语序调整。例如：

1. Where water resources are plentiful, hydroelectric power stations are being built in large numbers.

哪里水源充足，就在哪里修建大批的水电站。

2. Where you find high wages, you will find high prices.

3. Wherever he happens to be, John can make himself at home.

2.2　译为汉语其他状语从句

英语中的地点状语从句除翻译为汉语中的地点状语从句外，还可译为汉语中表示因果、条件或假设等关系的状语从句。例如：

1. Where much is alleged, something must be true.

由于大家都这么说，想必有些是真的。

在上面的例子中，"where" 所引导的地点状语从句和主句间是因果关系，因而被译为了汉语中的原因状语从句。再如：

2. Where usage is so undecided, it would be presumptuous to favor one over the other.

3. Birth is nothing where virtue is not.

4. Where a vessel has vertical sides, the pressure on the bottom is equal to the height of the liquid times its density.

5. Love is a feeling or emotion…like hate, jealousy, hunger, thirst…necessary where rationality alone would not suffice to carry the day.

第3节　原因状语从句

英语原因状语从句一般可直接译为汉语中的原因状语，但英语作为形合性语言，其原因状语从句的位置比较灵活，它可位于句首或句尾，而汉语则一般按照先因后果的逻辑顺序组句。例如：

1. As he didn't know much English, he looked up the word in the dictionary.
由于英语懂得不多，他在词典中查阅这个单词。

2. Now that the weather has cleared up, we can start our journey.

3. There will be a lot of people coming from outside and that will be a big challenge since Greenlandic culture has been isolated.

4. It is frequently said that computers solve problems only because they are "programmed" to do so.

一些英语中的原因状语从句，如果其重心在原因部分，则翻译时可把原句中的原因状语从句译为汉语中的主句，原句中的主句译为汉语中的结果状语从句。例如：

5. Because he was convinced of the accuracy of this fact, he stuck to his opinion.
他深信这件事正确可靠，因此坚持己见。

6. Pure iron is not used in industry because it is too soft.

此外，汉语中的因果关系往往是暗含在句子中的，因而英语原因状语从句在译为汉语时，往往可以省译连词，译为汉语不带关联词且内含因果关系的并列分句。例如

7. He was not nervous at all, because he was ready.
他胸有成竹，一点儿也不紧张。
在上句中，省译了连词"because"，译文更加流畅。再如：

8. Because the earth is the only home of our human beings, everyone in the world has the responsibility to protect the environment.

9. Since the electrical inventions which Edison had given us were very important, we could not live without them… not for one minute.

第4节 条件状语从句

英语中的条件状语从句，无论其位于句首还是句尾，一般可以译为汉语中的位于句首的条件从句。例如：

1. We won't be able to go there on foot in case it rains.

要是下雨，咱们就不能步行上那儿去了。

在上例中，英文条件句位于句尾，译为汉语时，根据逻辑关系，其被调整到了句首。再如：

2. If you think American cooking means opening a package and tossing contents into the microwave, think again.

3. Should there be an urgent situation, press the red button to switch off the electricity.

当英语中条件状语从句表示弱化的条件时，需译为汉语中的补充成分，且位于句尾。例如：

4. You'll have some money by then, if you last the week out.

到那时你该有点钱了，如果你能度过这星期的话。

在上面的例子中，"if"引导的条件句是对主句的语义补充说明，因而不用调整语序。再如：

5. Any body above the earth will fall unless it is supported by an upward force equal to its weight.

6. Many people like him plan to return to get their degrees, even if few actually do.

此外，将一些英语条件状语从句译为汉语中不含关联词、内含条件关系的句子，可使译文言简意赅，符合汉语的表达习惯。例如：

7. If the temperature drops to zero degree centigrade, water freezes.

水在摄氏零度结冰。

上例把英文主从复合句压缩为了汉语简单句，表达更加流畅。再如：

8. If you melt two or more metals together, you can get a new metal.

第5节 让步状语从句

英语让步状语从句一般可直接译为汉语表让步的分句,并根据汉语的表达习惯在需要时进行语序调整。例如:

1. While we can not see the air, we can feel it.
我们虽然看不见空气,但能感觉到它。

2. I still think that you made a mistake while I admit what you say.

3. Even though the majority of the population now lives in cities, much of New Zealand's art, literature, film and humor has rural themes.

以"how/wh-+ever, no matter how/wh-+ever, whether"为引导词的让步状语从句,一般为"无条件"的条件分句,即在任何条件下都会产生同样的结果,它可译为汉语中的"无论,不论……"句型。例如:

4. He got the same result whichever way he did the experiment.
不论用什么方法做实验,他所得到的结果都一致。

5. Whether the characters portrayed are taken from real life or are purely imaginary, they may become our companions and friends.

6. While one finds company in himself and his pursuits, he cannot feel old, no matter what his years may be.

第6节 目的状语从句

英语中的目的状语从句译为汉语时位置比较灵活,既可前置又可后置。例如:

1. The travel plan was cancelled in order that the spread of SARS could be prevented.

为了防止非典的传染,这次旅行计划被取消了。

2. He pushed open the door gently and stole out of the room for fear that he should awake her.

3. We strive to improve our performance as professional conference organizers, making administration details easy so that delegates feel motivated and leave with positive perceptions about the client and sponsors.

4. He is planning to make this speech in order that we might have a better understanding of the vicissitude of the international situation.

第 7 节 结果状语从句

英语中的结果状语从句一般可译为汉语中表示结果的分句，或者省译连词，译为汉语中不含关联词但内含因果关系的并列分句。例如：

1. He never played with the children that a quarrel did not follow.
   他跟孩子们玩耍，结果总是吵架。

2. He made a wrong decision, so that half of his lifetime was wasted.

3. Peter is such a nice boy that he is loved by everybody.

4. Such was his anxiety that he couldn't stop trembling.

第 8 节　方式状语从句

英语中表示方式的状语从句通常位于主句之后，译为汉语时往往置于主语和谓语之间作为方式状语。例如：

1. Please do exactly as your doctor says.

   务请按照医生的吩咐行事。

2. Mary does not bother about trifles the way her sister does.

但 as... so... 结构，或 as if, as though 等引导的方式状语从句，一般为蕴涵隐喻的谚语或习语，翻译起来位置比较灵活。例如：

3. The clouds disappeared as if by magic.

   那些云团消失得无影无踪，如同被魔力驱散了。

4. As the twig is bent, so the tree is inclined.

练习

一、翻译下列句子，注意其中状语从句的翻译。

1. Please turn off the light when you leave the room.

2. When we met each other for the second time, I found that she looked older than she was.

3. When you write less, your composition will become worse.

4. Almost all large and small stores in every part of the country wait and prepare for the Christmas and Easter holidays when they expect to "do a landoffice business."

5. He was on the verge of losing his temper with his wife when she uttered a cry.

6. We can't start the job until we have the approval from the authority concerned.

7. When bad men combine, good men must associate.

8. Not until we have detailed studies of the present movement of traffic and have a clearer idea of how many people wish to travel, where they want to go, at what time of day and how quickly... not until then can we begin to plan a proper transportation system for the future.

9. Where there is clean air and water, there are people who live a long life.

10. The materials are excellent for use where the value of the workpieces is not high.

11. Light is the task where many share the toil.

12. Where lobbyists used to avoid notoriety and preferred to work behind scenes, many today seek publicity as a useful tool.

13. As the moon's gravity is only about 1/6 of the gravity of the earth, a 200-pound man weighs only 33 pounds on the moon.

14. 2010 Guangzhou Asian Games went on smoothly, because over five hundred thousand volunteers took an active part in the service for the games.

15. As families move away from their stable community, their friends of many years, and their extended family relationships, the informal flow of information is cut off.

16. It can, however, only do so if its role in international economic co-operation is recognized and its outstretched hand accepted.

17. If the epidemic cannot be controlled effectively, the whole country will come into chaos.

18. No doubt I could earn something if I had really meant to.

19. Granted that you don't like the proposal, you shouldn't have rejected it without consulting others.

20. Every Sunday now, the residents of this town in southwest Spain... young and old... do what needs to be done, whether it is cleaning the streets, raking the leaves, unclogging culverts or planting trees in the park.

21. We are all, whatever part of the world we come from, persuaded that our own nation is superior to all others.

22. He sent a bunch of flowers each day in order that he could win her love.

23. The book was so boring that he gave up reading it half way through.

24. We turned up the radio, so that everyone heard the news.

25. They treat the black boy as if he were an animal.

二、翻译下面的段落，注意其中状语从句的翻译。

Though fond of many acquaintances, I desire an intimacy only with a few. The Man in Black, whom I have often mentioned, is one whose friendship I could wish to acquire, because he possesses my esteem. His manners, it is true, are tinctured with some strange inconsistencies, and he may be justly termed a humorist in a nation of humorists. Though he is generous even to profusion, he affects to be thought a prodigy of parsimony and prudence; though his conversation be replete with the most sordid and selfish maxims, his heart is dilated with the most unbounded love. I have known him profess himself a man-hater, while his cheek was glowing with compassion; and, while his looks were softened into pity, I have heard him use the language of the most unbounded ill-nature. Some affect humanity and tenderness, others boast of having such dispositions from Nature; but he is the only man I ever knew who seemed ashamed of his natural benevolence. He takes as much pain to hide his feelings, as any hypocrite would to conceal his indifference; but on every unguarded moment the mask drops off, and reveals him to the most superficial observer.

第 16 章

名词性从句

英语名词性从句包括主语从名、宾语从句、表语从句和同位语从句等。翻译的时候,大多数可以按照原文的句子顺序翻译成相应的汉语句子。但是,有时候,可以用换序法、分译法、合译法等其他翻译方法来对其灵活处理。

第 1 节 主 语 从 句

1.1 由代词或连词引导的主语从句

由代词"what, which, how, why, where, who, whatever, whoever, whenever, wherever"以及连词"that, whether"等引导的主语从句,一般在翻译时不需做位置调整,保留原文的语序,译在句首,作为主从复合句的主语。例如:

1. Whatever he saw and heard on his trip gave him a very deep impression.
他此行所见所闻都给他留下了深刻的印象。

2. Why so many low-income students fall from the college ranks is a question without a simple answer.

3. How and when human language developed and whether animals such as chimpanzees and gorillas can develop a more elaborate system of communication are issues at present being researched, but as yet little understood.

4. That our environment has little, if anything, to do with our abilities, characteristics and behavior is central to this theory.

1.2 由"it"引导的主语从句

英语中有许多用"it"作形式主语的主语从句。这时,主语从句在翻译时位置比较灵活,可前置或后置,但后置情况较多,特别是当主句表达作者的观点、态度时,后置居多。例如:

1. It seemed inconceivable that the pilot could have survived the crash.
驾驶员在飞机坠毁之后,竟然还能活着,这看来是不可想象的。

上句中,"it"所引导的主语从句表达了说话者的观点,因而译为汉语时放在了句尾,并用"这"对叙事部分,即"that"引导的从句进行了复指。再如:

2. It is common knowledge that, to master any language, especially one's mother tongue, one must begin from childhood.

3. It was therefore surprising and somewhat disappointing that, upon coming to China to teach writing at a university in mid-2006, I discovered that the average Chinese learners was far more interested in *King Kong* than the subtle yet profoundly insightful poetry of the Tang Dynasty genius Li Bai.

4. It is certain that technology, especially computer technology, will rule our lives to a greater and greater degree.

第 2 节 宾 语 从 句

2.1 由代词或连词引导的宾语从句

用 "what, how, when, which, why, whether, that" 等代词或连词引导的宾语从句，翻译成汉语的时候，一般采用顺译法，不需要改变它在原句中的顺序。例如：

1. They would be proud to proclaim that they knew only English and some even felt somewhat contemptuous of the Chinese culture.

他们非常骄傲地宣称自己只懂英文，一些人甚至对中国文化抱有鄙夷的态度。

2. If ever I become a parent, I will bring my children camping. I will show them that cooking food in a mess tin over a campfire is fun. I will teach them that there is nothing dirty about lying on a sleeping bag over grass.

3. At the same time, however, technology has also enabled fishermen to reach far deeper than ever before, into areas where bottom trawls can destroy in minutes what has taken nature hundreds and in some cases thousands of years to build.

4. The emergence of China as a potential political and economic superpower has driven home to these parents that becoming bilingual will not only enhance their children's employment prospects, but also make them a man of two cultures.

5. The distinctive culture's core to what makes New Zealand a great place to live.

2.2 用 "it" 作形式宾语的宾语从句

当 "it" 作形式宾语时，that 所引导的宾语从句一般也按英语原文顺序翻译，但通常 "it" 不需翻译。例如：

1. I made it clear to them that they must hand in their papers before 10 o'clock in the morning.

我向他们讲清楚了，他们必须在上午 10 时前交论文。

2. We consider it absolutely necessary that we should open our door to the outside world.

3. You have all heard it repeated that men of science work by means of induction and deduction, that by the help of these operations, they, in a sort of sense, manage to extract from nature certain natural laws, and that out of these by some special skill of their own, they build up their theories.

第 3 节 表 语 从 句

英语表语从句在汉译时一般采用顺译法，即保留原文的语序。例如：

1. The result of invention of steam engine was that human power was replaced by mechanical power.

蒸汽机发明的结果是机械力代替了人力。

2. That is why heat can melt ice, vaporize water and cause bodies to expand.

3. The basic problem is they thought of transport alone, without considering all these other effects.

4. What we should like to know is whether life originated as the result of some amazing accidents or succession of coincidences, or whether it is the normal event for inanimate matter to produce life in due course, when the physical environment is suitable.

5. What many undergraduates do not know… and what so many of their professors have been unable to tell them… is how valuable the most fundamental gift of the humanities will turn out to be.

第4节 同位语从句

英语同位语从句的翻译方法比较灵活，可以顺译、译为定语或分译等。

4.1 顺译

当同位语从句所修饰的名词含有动作意味时，可以把其转译为动词或增译与其搭配的动词，把同位语从句译为宾语，按照原文顺序翻译，使语言流畅。例如：

1. He expressed the hope that he would come over to visit China again.

他表示希望能再来中国访问。

在上面的例子中，同位语从句所修饰的名词"hope"含有动作意味，因而转译为了动词，同位语从句语序不变，译为了其宾语。再如：

2. An order has been given that the researchers who are now in the sky-lab should be sent back.

3. But, until now, there has been no evidence that any bird could make the big leap to associating one sound exclusively with one object or quality.

4. A year later, the father received a letter that one of his lost ships had been found and had arrived filled with merchandise for him.

4.2 译为定语

英语中较简单的同位语从句在译为汉语时，可以将其放在所修饰名词的前面，相当于前置的修饰语。例如：

1. The rumor that he releases the news is groundless.

他泄露消息的谣传是毫无根据的。

在上面的例子中，同位语从句是对"the rumor"的限定、解释，汉译时被前置为定语。再如：

2. We know the fact that bodies possess weight.

3. Don't cherish the illusion that your father will always support you financially.

4. The hypothesis was made that one's thought was to some extent controlled by the language he speaks.

4.3 译为独立句子

英语中的不少同位语从句可译为独立句子,置于句首。在这种情况下,主句往往可译为"这……"的句子以对前置的同位语从句进行复指。例如:

1. The dictum that the style is the man is known to most of us.
文如其人,这句名言是我们大多数人都熟悉的。

2. The statement that most people are for this proposal is confirmed by a survey conducted recently.

3. That aspect has to be weighed against the fact that they might not help your career plans.

4.4 使用分号、破折号或"即""那就是"

英语较长的同位语从句在译为汉语时,可以使用分号、破折号或"即""那就是"把其与主句分开,即进行分译。例如:

1. One month later, Einstein put forward another theory that matter and energy were not completely different.
一个月后,爱因斯坦提出了另一种理论:物质和能量并非完全不同。

2. He believed in a hypothesis first put forth by Darwin that humans and chimpanzees share an evolutionary ancestor.

3. Not long ago, the scientists made an exciting discovery that this waste material could be turned into plastics.

4. Unfortunately, Plato's analogy misses an important characteristic of memory, namely it is selective.

5. Finally, Einstein arrived at a conclusion that maximum speed in the universe is that of light.

6. A century ago, Freud formulated his revolutionary theory that dreams were the disguised shadows of our unconscious desires and fears.

练习

一、翻译下列含有名词性从句的句子。

1. How well the prediction will be validated by later performance depends upon the amount, reliability, and appropriateness of the information used and on the skill and wisdom with which it is interpreted.

2. It is a matter of common experience that bodies are lighter in water than they are in air.

3. It is often said that wide reading is the best alternative course of action but even here it is necessary to make some kinds of selection.

4. It was evident that to answer the letter he needed something more than goodwill, ink, and paper.

5. Parents are required by law to see that their children receive full-time education, at school or elsewhere, between the ages of 5 and 16 in England, Scotland and Wales and 4 and 16 in Northern Ireland.

6. He said that part of the problem was that when it set the targets, the European Union was trying desperately to solve the problem of rising transportation emissions.

7. It is virtually impossible to imagine that universities, hospitals, large businesses or even science and technology could have come into being without cities to support them.

8. Nutritional experiments have made it evident that vitamins are indispensable for one's growth and health.

9. The most important part of any therapy is not what you understand or what you

talk about, but what you do.

10. What happens is that the hotter people get, physiologically, with mental stress, the more likely they are to blow apart with some heart problem.

11. Galileo's greatest glory was that in 1609 he was the first person to turn the newly invented telescope on the heavens to prove that the planets revolve around the sun rather than around the earth.

12. However, the writing of chemical symbols in the form of an equation does not give any assurance that the reaction shown will actually occur.

13. She had no idea why she thought of him suddenly.

14. There is a possibility that he is a spy.

15. Experts said the new study is one more evidence that physical exercise can reduce iron in human body.

16. The rumor that he was arrested was unfounded.

17. There was the possibility that a small electrical spark might accidentally bypass the most carefully planned circuit.

18. This does not alter the fact that that is, from a practical point view, a best solution.

19. Most often this advice includes suggestions that we should eat right, exercise, take vitamins and get a pet.

20. Arguing from the view that humans are different from animals in every relevant respect, extremists of this kind think that animals lie outside the area of moral choice.

二、翻译下面的段落，注意其中名词性从句的翻译。

To be truly happy is a question of how we begin and not of how we end, of what we want and not of what we have. An aspiration is a joy forever, a possession as solid as a landed estate, a fortune which we can never exhaust and which gives us year by year a revenue of pleasurable activity. To have many of these is to be spiritually rich. Life is only a very dull and ill-directed theater unless we have some interests in the piece; and to those who have neither art nor science, the world is mere arrangement of colors, or a rough footway where they may break their shins. It is in virtue of his own desires and curiosities that any man continues to exist with even patience, that he is charmed by the look of things and people, and that he wakens every morning with a renewed appetite for work and pleasure. Desire and curiosity are the two eyes through which he sees the world in the most enchanted colors: it is they that make women beautiful or fossils interesting; and the man may squander his estate and come to beggary, but if he keeps these two amulets he is still rich in the possibilities of pleasure.

附录一

英译汉篇章练习

1. Washington's Address to His Troops

The time is now near at hand which must probably determine whether Americans are to be freemen or slaves; whether they are to have any property they can call their own; whether their houses and farms are to be pillaged and destroyed, and themselves consigned to a state of wretchedness from which no human efforts will deliver them. The fate of unborn millions will now depend, under God, on the courage and conduct of this army. Our cruel and unrelenting enemy leaves us only the choice of a brave resistance or the most abject submission. We have, therefore, to resolve to conquer or to die.

Our own, our country's honor, calls upon us for a vigorous and manly exertion; and if we now shamefully fail, we shall become infamous to the whole world. Let us then rely on the goodness of our cause, and the aid of the Supreme Being, in whose hands victory is, to animate and encourage us to great and noble actions. The eyes of all our countrymen are now upon us, and we shall have their blessings and praises, if happily we are the instruments of saving them from the tyranny meditated against them. Let us, therefore, animate and encourage each other, and show the whole world that a free man contending for liberty on his own ground is superior to any slavish mercenary on Earth.

Liberty, property, life, and honor are all at stake. Upon your courage and conduct rest the hopes of our bleeding and insulted country. Our wives, children, and parents expect safety from us, only; and they have every reason to believe that Heaven will crown with success so just a cause. The enemy will endeavor to intimidate by show and appearance; but remember, they have been repulsed on various occasions by a few brave Americans. Their cause is bad... their men are conscious of it; and if opposed with firmness and coolness on their first onset, with our advantage of works, and knowledge of the ground, the victory is most assuredly ours. Every good soldier will be silent and attentive... wait for orders, and reserve his fire until he is sure of doing execution.

2. A Letter to His Son

You must study to be frank with the world. Frankness is the child of honesty and courage. Say just what you mean to do, on every occasion, and take it for granted that you mean to do right. If a friend asks a favor, you should grant it, if it is reasonable; if not, tell him plainly why you cannot; you would wrong him and wrong yourself by equivocation of any kind.

Never do a wrong thing to make a friend or keep one; the man who requires you to do so is dearly purchased at a sacrifice. Deal kindly but firmly with all your classmates; you will find it the policy which wears best. Above all, do not appear to others what you are not.

If you have any fault to find with anyone, tell him, not others, of what you complain; there is no more dangerous experiment than that of undertaking to be one thing before a man's face and another behind his back. We should live, act, and say nothing to the injury of anyone. It is not only for the best as a matter of principle, but it is the path of peace and honor.

In regard to duty, let me, in conclusion of this hasty letter, inform you that nearly a hundred years ago there was a day of remarkable gloom and darkness,... still known as "the dark day,"... a day when the light or the sun was slowly extinguished, as if by an eclipse.

Duty, then, is the sublimest word in our language. Do your duty in all things like the old Puritan. You cannot do more; you should never wish to do less. Never let your mother or me wear one gray hair for any lack on your part.

3. Why Women Live Longer than Men

If you could take an immense group snapshot of everyone in the United States today, it would contain six million more females than males. In this country, women outlast men by about seven years. Throughout the modern world, cultures are different, diets are different, ways of life and causes of death are different, but one thing is the same... women outlive men.

It starts before birth. At conception, male fetuses outnumber female by about 110 to 100; at birth the ratio has already fallen to about 105 boys to every 100 girls. By age 30, there are only enough men left to match the number of women. Then women start building a lead. Beyond age 80, there are nearly twice as many women as men.

"If you look at the top ten or 12 causes of death," says Deborah Wingard, an epidemiologist at the University of California at San Diego, "every single one kills more men." She rattles off one melancholy fate after another... heart disease, lung cancer, homicide, cirrhosis of the liver and pneumonia. Each kills men at roughly twice the rate it does women.

A century ago American men outnumbered and outlived the women. But in the 20th century, women began living longer, primarily because pregnancy and children had become less dangerous. The gap grew steadily. In 1946, for the first time ever in the United States, females outnumbered males.

4. The Forty Most Important Minutes Each Day: Are You Using Them Well?

I had a teacher whose advice to us students was that for memorization purposes, there are forty minutes each day in which our memory is vastly more receptive than it is during the other 23 hours and 20 minutes. This 40-minute "super memory" period is divided into two parts: the 20 minutes before we sleep, and the 20 minutes after we first awake.

The theory supporting this is pretty simple. First, the last information you input into your brain before a good night's sleep has a better chance of taking root than information acquired during the hustle bustle of normal daily routine; and, second, your mind is free of distraction when you first awake in the morning... so more receptive to inputs, like a blank slate. The technique really works, but like many things, it takes practice and discipline to hone and perfect it.

As far as language study goes, it's not only useful for memorizing vocabulary. It's also a very useful window of time in which to listen to the language you're studying, even as background noise, and even if it's at a level you find difficult to comprehend. It might be audio language study aids, or just radio, TV or whatever.

Beyond our years of formal education, memory skills are hugely important in any career. How many times have you heard a speaker read their speech from a prepared text, or read the word-by-word content of a PowerPoint presentation as they present each slide? These are annoying, distracting, boring, and ineffective ways of communicating. They are almost guaranteed to lose the audience's close attention and interest, let alone persuade or inspire anyone to do anything. And yet lots of people still make this mistake.

If you use the "forty minute" technique, you may not succeed in memorizing your presentation contents on a 100% word-by-word basis, but you'll be familiar enough that you can spend much more time making eye contact with your audience. You will engage them in the process, while glancing at your text instead of staring at it. This will also free up your hands and arms to add some emphasis through gesture.

5. North Korea's Nuclear Issue

Members of the United Nations Security Council are considering new sanctions for North Korea in reaction to its sixth and most powerful nuclear test.

However, experts say the support of China is critical to increase pressure on the government of North Korean leader Kim Jong Un.

China's Foreign Minister Wang Yi said Thursday, "The U. N. Security Council should respond further and take necessary measures."

But, Wang said "sanctions and pressure" must be tied to "dialogue and negotiations." China has said that increased restrictions will not ease tensions on the Korean Peninsula.

U. S. President Donald Trump spoke to Chinese President Xi Jinping about North Korea on Wednesday. Trump said Xi agreed on the need to answer North Korea's nuclear test, saying, "He does not want to see what is happening there either."

On Monday, U. S. Ambassador to the United Nations Nikki Haley said the 15-member UN Security Council would negotiate a version of a resolution to place new sanctions on North Korea. She said the U. S. would seek a vote by Monday.

On August 5, the UN Security Council approved resolution 2371. It came as the result of two long-range missile tests that North Korea carried out in July. The UN Security Council barred North Korea from exporting coal, iron, lead and seafood, along with other restrictions. The measures were aimed at cutting about one-third of North Korea's $3 billion in export income.

However, now there are calls to cut North Korea's fuel imports in an effort to build pressure on its leaders.

6. Doubt About Yourself?

Unrelenting self-criticism often goes hand in hand with depression and anxiety, and it may even predict depression. In a study of 107 patients in the latest issue of *Comprehensive Psychiatry*, David M. Dunkley at Jewish General Hospital in Montreal and colleagues found that those who were most self-critical were the most likely to be depressed and have difficulties in relationships four years later, even if they weren't depressed to begin with.

Self-criticism is also a factor in eating disorders, self-mutilation and body dysmorphic disorder... that is, preoccupation with one's perceived physical flaws. "We have expanded what we expect of material success and physical appearance so that it's completely unrealistic," says Robert L. Leahy, a psychiatrist and director of the American Institute for Cognitive Therapy in New York.

Many people's Inner Critic makes an appearance early in life and is such a constant companion that it's part of their personality. Psychologists say that children, particularly those with a genetic predisposition to depression, may internalize and exaggerate the expectations of parents or peers or society. One theory is that self-criticism is anger turned inward, when sufferers are filled with hostility but too afraid and insecure to let it out. Other theories hold that people who scold themselves are acting out guilt or shame or subconsciously shielding themselves against criticism from others: You can't tell me anything I don't already tell myself, in even harsher terms.

7. Primary Health Care in Developing Countries

In poor countries people are living longer and healthier lives than ever. Since 2000 child mortality has fallen by almost half. The rate of new HIV/AIDS infections has dropped by 40%. About 7 million deaths from malaria have been prevented.

Yet there is much more to be done. By one measure, the World Health Organization reckons about 400m people still have no access to primary care... the basic form of medicine that should be at the forefront of any well-run health system. The real figure is probably much higher. And even for those fortunate enough to see a general practitioner, or more usually a semi-trained medic or quack, treatment is often dire.

The poor state of primary care will matter even more as the burden of disease in poor countries comes to resemble than in rich ones, shifting from infectious diseases to chronic conditions. By 2020 non-communicable diseases will account for about 70% of deaths in developing countries. But the majority of people with high blood pressure, diabetes or depression does not get effective treatment... and may not even know they have a problem. They deserve better.

Primary health care is not flashy, but it works. It is the central nervous system of a country's medical services... monitoring the general health of communities, treating chronic conditions and providing day-to-day relief. It can ensure that an infectious disease does not become an epidemic. Before the Ebola outbreak of

2014, nearly half of Liberians could not afford primary care and the deadly virus spread quickly. In parts of West Africa with better primary care, it was more easily contained.

8. Machine Time

In an essay entitled "Making It in America," the author Adam Davidson relates a joke from cotton country about just how much a modern textile mill has been automated: The average mill has only two employees today, "a man and a dog. The man is there to feed the dog and the dog is there to keep the man away from the machines."

Davidson's article is one of a number of pieces that have recently appeared making the point that the reason we have such stubbornly high unemployment and declining middle-class incomes today is also because of the advances in both globalization and the information technology revolution, which are more rapidly than ever replacing labor with machines or foreign workers.

In the past, workers with average skills, doing an average job, could earn an average lifestyle. But, today, average is officially over. Being average just won't earn you what it used to. It can't, when so many more employers have so much more access to so much more above average cheap foreign labor, cheap robotics, cheap software, cheap automation and cheap genius. Therefore, everyone needs to find their extra... their unique value contribution that makes them stand out in whatever their field of employment is.

Yes, new technology has been eating jobs forever, and always will. But there's been an acceleration. As Davidson notes, "In the 10 years ending in 2009, (U.S.) factories shed workers so fast that they erased almost all the gains of the previous 70 years; roughly one out of every three manufacturing jobs... about 6 million in total... disappeared."

9. Adolescence

The period of adolescence, i.e., the period between childhood and adulthood, may be long or short, depending on social expectations and on society's definition as to what constitutes maturity and adulthood. In primitive societies adolescence is frequently a relatively short period of time, while in industrial societies with patterns of prolonged education coupled with laws against child labor, the period of adolescence is much longer and may include most of the second decade of one's life. Furthermore, the length of the adolescent period and the definition of adulthood status may change in a given society as social and economic conditions change. Examples of this type of change are the disappearance of the frontier in the latter part of the nineteenth century in the United States, and more universally, the industrialization of an agricultural society.

In modern society, ceremonies for adolescence have lost their formal recognition and symbolic significance and there no longer is agreement as to what constitutes initiation ceremonies. Social ones have been replaced by a sequence of steps that lead to increased recognition and social status. For example, grade school graduation, high school graduation and college graduation constitute such a sequence, and while each step implies certain behavioral changes and social recognition, the significance of each depends on the socio-economic status and the educational ambition of the individual. Ceremonies for adolescence have also been replaced by legal definitions of status roles, right, privileges and responsibilities. It is during the nine years from the twelfth birthday to the twenty-first that the protective and restrictive aspects of childhood and minor status are removed and adult privileges and responsibilities are granted.

10. Smart Bin

A new "smart bin" could spell the end of environment-conscious families spending hours sorting tins, cartons, bottles, and cardboard for recycling. The invention, which automatically sorts rubbish into recycling categories, is being trialed in Poland and is set to go on sale in UK within a few years. The bin, designed by start-up company Bin. E, recognizes different types of waste via a system positioned inside the bin which uses sensors, image recognition and artificial intelligence. Once waste is placed inside, the camera and sensors identify its type and place it in one of the smaller bins. Then it compresses the waste so it occupies less space. News of the launch comes after this newspaper revealed that more than a million households are being forced to accept bin collections every three or four weeks, because councils are trying to force them to recycle more. Data compiled by *The Telegraph* has revealed at least 18 councils have moved or will shortly be moving to three-weekly rubbish collections, while a further three have adopted or are trialing four-weekly collections. While reducing general bin collections councils are increasing the frequency of recycling collections in a bid to change people's behaviour.

It is thought that the bin could be stocked by department stores such as John Lewis, which said it is introducing new hi-tech recycling bins to satisfy increasing customer appetite for them. Matt Thomas, utility buyer at John Lewis, said: "We've recently seen a jump in specialist bins sales, with a 25 percent increase in the last few months alone. We have noticed our customers are becoming more and more sustainability focused, opting for dual compartment recycling bins that make it far easier to recycle different types of waste."

11. About Reading

Sales of children's literature have risen by double digits in most of the past ten years, much faster than the growth of book sales overall. The number of children's titles has more than tripled since 2005. This partly reflects a growing demand for products aimed at indulged only-children. A cost-conscious reluctance to have more offspring, which was reinforced by the country's recently relaxed one-child policy, helped fuel that demand. The richer parents are, the more they splash out on children's books.

Booksellers see a huge moneymaking opportunity. Most publishers of literature for adults now offer children's titles too. Around half of the 100 best-selling books last year were for youngsters... a higher share than in Britain or America. There is a growing variety of genres. Picture books for under-fives have been taking off; fiction for older teenagers is thriving.

Unsurprisingly, given the huge emphasis in China that is placed on passing exams, many titles aim purely to teach facts. Parents like to buy non-fiction, even for children still learning to read. Some books... printed on paperboard and intended mainly for under-twos... aim to teach the Roman alphabet to infants. Volumes for toddlers with titles such as "How to Be a Meteorologist" and "Superstars of Science" do well.

12. Energy in China

Energy is an essential material basis for human survival and development. Over the entire history of mankind, each and every significant step in the progress of human civilization has been accompanied by energy innovations and substitutions. The development and utilization of energy has enormously boosted the development of the world economy and human society. Over more than 100 years in the past, developed countries have completed their industrialization, consuming an enormous quantity of natural resources, especially energy resources, in the process. Today, some developing countries are ushering in their own era of industrialization, and an increase of energy consumption is inevitable for their economic and social development.

China is the largest developing country in the world, and developing its economy and eliminating poverty will, for a long time to come, remain the main tasks for the Chinese government and the Chinese people. Since the late 1970s, China, as the fastest growing developing country, has scored brilliant achievements in its economy and society that have attracted worldwide attention, successfully blazed the trail of socialism with Chinese characteristics, and made significant contributions to world development and prosperity.

China is now the world's second-large energy producer and consumer. The sustained growth of energy supply has provided an important support for the country's economic growth and social progress, while the rapid expansion of energy consumption has created a vast scope for the global energy market. As an irreplaceable component of the world energy market, China plays an increasingly important role in maintaining global energy security.

13. Tragic Myth

Those who have never had the experience of having to see at the same time that they also longed to transcend all seeing will scarcely be able to imagine how definitely and clearly these two processes coexist and are felt at the same time, as one contemplates the tragic myth. But all truly aesthetic spectators will confirm that among the peculiar effects of tragedy this coexistence is the most remarkable. Now transfer this phenomenon of the aesthetic spectator into an analogous process in the tragic artist, and you will have understood the genesis of the tragic myth. With the Apollonian art sphere he shares the complete pleasure in mere appearance and in seeing, yet at the same time he negates this pleasure and finds a still higher satisfaction in the destruction of the visible world of mere appearance.

The content of the tragic myth is, first of all, an epic event and the glorification of the fighting hero. But what is the origin of this enigmatic trait that the suffering and the fate of the hero, the most painful triumphs, the most agonizing oppositions of motives, in short, the exemplification of this wisdom of Silenus, or, to put it aesthetically, that which is ugly and disharmonic, is represented ever anew in such countless forms and with such a distinct preference... and precisely in the most fruitful and youthful period of a people? Surely a higher pleasure must be perceived in all this.

14. Pasterski

Being compared to geniuses like Stephen Hawking and Albert Einstein is not something that happens to the average person. So when we tell you that Sabrina Gonzalez Pasterski is far from your average human, we mean it.

At the age of just 23, Paterski has already accomplished more than most of us ever will in our lifetime. When she was only 14-years-old, the Chicago native, constructed her own single engine airplane by herself. If that wasn't impressive enough she then flew it across Lake Michigan, becoming the youngest person to ever fly their own plane. The whole venture took two years to complete, and she documented the entire experience on YouTube. She then graduated from Illinois Mathematics and Science Academy in 2010 and enrolled with the prestigious Massachusetts Institute of Technology. After just three years at MIT she has already achieved the highest possible grade point average of 5.0. She is now working towards her doctorate at the world renowned Harvard University, with full academic freedom and no interference from staff.

Once again she is only 23-years-old. What's even more remarkable is that she is no longer interested in building planes but has turned her attention to physics; namely black holes and how gravity affects space and time... hence the Einstein and Hawking comparisons. She particularly wants to study "quantum gravity," where she will attempt to understand the link between gravities within the context of quantum physics. If her research proves successful, discoveries in this area could vastly change the way we understand the universe. During an interview earlier this year she said, "Be optimistic about what you believe you can do. When you're little, you say a lot of things about what you'll do or be when you're older... I think it's important not to lose sight of those dreams."

15. Kobe Bryant

One of the toughest games I remember playing against Kobe happened in Boston. I think he made seven or eight shots in a row on me. So we come into the huddle during a timeout and the coach is looking at me with a face that I knew meant he wanted me to switch off of Kobe. And the rest of the guys on the team could see what was happening and they were looking at me too. Finally they bring up that maybe we should switch and put a different guy on him, and I yelled, "Hell no! I'm going to guard him! I got this!"

He ended up missing the last nine shots of that game with me on him, and we won. But the stat sheet is still vivid in my mind. Kobe took 47 shots. Forty-seven. No one has ever taken 47 shots on me. Most games a team will get up 81 to 89 shots.

What you have to understand about Kobe's game is that by taking that many shots, he's meticulously wearing down the defender until he breaks them. He's made a career out of making guys lose confidence in their defense and then continuing to attack them. He's won five rings doing that.

If you want to have any defensive success against Kobe, you can't break. That's much easier said than done.

16. Companionship of Books

A man may usually be known by the books he reads as well as by the company he keeps; for there is a companionship of books as well as of men; and one should always live in the best company, whether it be of books or of men.

A good book may be among the best of friends. It is the same today as it always was, and it will never change. It is the most patient and cheerful of companions. It does not turn its back upon us in times of adversity or distress. It always receives us with the same kindness; amusing and instructing us in youth, and comforting and consoling us in age.

Men often discover their affinity to each other by the mutual love they have for a book just as two persons sometimes discover a friend by the admiration which both entertain for a third. There is an old proverb, "Love me, love my dog." But there is more wisdom in this: "Love me, love my book." The book is a truer and higher bond of union. Men can think, feel, and sympathize with each other through their favorite author. They live in him together, and he in them.

A good book is often the best urn of a life enshrining the best that life could think out; for the world of a man's life is, for the most part, but the world of his thoughts. Thus the best books are treasuries of good words, the golden thoughts, which, remembered and cherished, become our constant companions and comforters.

Books possess an essence of immortality. They are by far the most lasting products of human effort. Temples and statues decay, but books survive. Time is of no account with great thoughts, which are as fresh today as when they first passed through their author's minds, ages ago. What was then said and thought still speaks to us as vividly as ever from the printed page. The only effects of time have been to sift out the bad products; for nothing in literature can long survive but what is really good.

Books introduce us into the best society; they bring us into the presence of the greatest minds that have ever lived. We hear what they said and did; we see them as if they were really alive; we sympathize with them, enjoy with them, grieve with them; their experience becomes ours, and we feel as if we were acting with them in the scenes which they describe.

The great and good do not die, even in this world. Embalmed in books, their spirits walk abroad. The book is a living voice. It is an intellect to which one still listens.

17. Humanity

The higher animals engage in individual fights, but never in organized masses. Man is the only animal that deals in that atrocity of atrocities, war. He is the only one that gathers his brethren about him and goes forth in cold blood and with calm pulse to exterminate his kind. He is the only animal that for sordid wages will march out, as the Hessians did in our Revolution, and as the boyish Prince Napoleon did in the Zulu war, and help to slaughter strangers of his own species who have done him no harm and with whom he has no quarrel.

Man is the only animal that robs his helpless fellow of his country, takes possession of it and drives him out of it or destroys him. Man has done these in all the ages. There is not an acre of ground on the globe that is in possession of its rightful owner, or that has not been taken away from owner after owner, cycle after cycle, by force and bloodshed.

Man is the only slave. And he is the only animal who enslaves. He has always been a slave in one form or another, and has always held other slaves in bondage under him in one way or another. In our day he is always some man's slave for wages, and does that man's work; and this slave has other slaves under him for minor wages, and they do his work. The higher animals are the only ones who exclusively do their own work and provide their own living.

Man is the only patriot. He sets himself apart in his own country, under his own flag, and sneers at the other nations, and keeps multitudinous uniformed assassins on hand at heavy expense to grab slices of other people's countries, and keep them from grabbing slices of his. And in the intervals between campaigns, he washes the blood off his hands and works for the universal brotherhood of man, with his mouth.

18. Commencement Speech

Rain, somebody said, is like confetti from heaven. So even the heavens are celebrating this morning, joining the rest of us at this wonderful commencement ceremony.

Before we go any further, graduates, you have an important task to perform because behind you are your parents and guardians. Two or three or four years ago they drove into Cardigan, dropped you off, help you get settled, and then turned around and drove back out the gates. It was an extraordinary sacrifice for them. They drove down the trail of tears back to an emptier and lonelier house. They did that because the decision about your education, they knew, was about you. It was not about them. That sacrifice and others they made have brought you to this point. But this morning is not just about you, it is also about them. So I hope you will stand up and turn around and give them a great round of applause, please.

Now when somebody asked me how the remarks at Cardigan went, I will be able to say they were interrupted by applause.

Congratulations class of 2017! You've reached an important milestone. An important stage of your life is behind you. I'm sorry to be the one to tell you it is the easiest stage of your life, but it is in the books. Now while you've been at Cardigan, you have all been a part of an important international community as well, and I think that needs to be particularly recognized.

Now around country today at colleges, high schools, middle schools, commencement speakers are standing before impatient graduates, and they are almost always saying the same things. They will say that today is a commencement exercise. It is a beginning, not an end. You should look forward and I think that is true enough.

19. A Harvard Speech by He Jiang

Despite the knowledge we have amassed, we haven't been so successful in deploying it to where it's needed most. According to the World Bank, twelve percent of the world's population lives on less than $2 a day. Malnutrition kills more than 3 million children annually. Three hundred million people are afflicted by malaria globally. All over the world, we constantly see these problems of poverty, illness, and lack of resources impeding the flow of scientific information. Lifesaving knowledge we take for granted in the modern world is often unavailable in these underdeveloped regions. And in far too many places, people are still essentially trying to cure a spider bite with fire.

While studying at Harvard, I saw how scientific knowledge can help others in simple, yet profound ways. The bird flu pandemic in the 2000s looked to my village like a spell cast by demons. Our folk medicine didn't even have half-measures to offer. What's more, farmers didn't know the difference between common cold and flu; they didn't understand that the flu was much more lethal than the common cold. Most people were also unaware that the virus could transmit across different animal species.

So when I realized that simple hygiene practices like separating different animal species could contain the spread of the disease, and that I could help make this knowledge available to my village, that was my first "Aha" moment as a budding scientist. But it was more than that: it was also a vital inflection point in my own ethical development, my own self-understanding as a member of the global community.

Harvard dares us to dream big, to aspire to change the world. Here on this Commencement Day, we are probably thinking of grand destinations and big adventures that await us. As for me, I am also thinking of the farmers in my village. My experience here reminds me how important it is for researchers to communicate our knowledge to those who need it. Because by using the science we already have, we could probably bring my village and thousands like it into the world you and I take for granted every day. And that's an impact every one of us can make!

20. Singles in China

With diners gathered around cauldrons of boiling soup, dropping meat and vegetables into the broth, hot pot is a quintessentially communal Chinese dish. But the country's dominant chain has a new weapon to attract single diners: stuffed bears.

The introduction of large plush toys to accompany solo diners in the 200 outlets of the Haidilao chain highlights the efforts of businesses in China to take advantage of a demographic shift creating a rising number of single consumers. "They help people feel less lonely," said Wang Ping, a waitress at a Haidilao in Shanghai, suggesting the Financial Times choose between a large teddy bear and a stuffed yellow chicken.

China's population of adults living alone has grown 16 percent since 2012 to reach 77 m, according to government statistics compiled by consultancy Euromonitor. By 2021, the number is set to rise to 92 m. The shift is driven by a trend towards later marriage in China, led by prosperous cities. In Shanghai, the average first marriage age for women has reached 30, up from 27 in 2011. Marriages are also shorter due to a doubling of the divorce rate in the past decade. 16 percent of China's urban population now lives alone, according to the Boston Consulting Group.

"The trend is accompanied by a profound change in people's perceptions of remaining single: the concept is no longer stigmatised," the group said in a recent report, meaning singles "dine, travel and pursue activities by themselves." Companies have responded to the trend, which mirrors demographic shifts already experienced by China's east Asian neighbours South Korea and Japan. Japanese chain Muji has introduced smaller rice cookers, ovens and kettles aimed at Chinese singles. Alibaba created Singles Day each November 11 as a celebration of the unattached lifestyle. It is now an annual consumer juggernaut, racking up RMB120.7 billion of sales in China in one day last year.

Asked on what they would most like to spend their time, China's singles chose watching films online and travelling "to make their plain and mundane lives more exciting," according to a recent report by consultancy Mintel. They are "less likely to travel for the connection with their family or shopping compared to married people," preferring sightseeing and experiencing local culture, the report adds.

Food delivery services have benefited from the trend. The sector saw 44 percent sales growth in China last year, according to consultancy Bain. Yang Gengshen, a spokesman for Ele.me, one of China's largest delivery services, which reported sales growth of 127 percent in the first half of this year, said: "In my experience, very few single people are willing to cook for themselves."

Meituan-Dianping, a restaurant review and food delivery company, said 65 percent of its orders came from unmarried customers, with fast food the most popular order for single consumers. "Single are the most important group of customers for us," said Wang Pu Zhong, general manager of Meituan's on-demand delivery service. "Chinese food is quite complicated... it takes a lot of time, so single people will think it is a waste of time compared to ordering take-out," he added.

Single eaters are a common sight in fast food restaurants and convenience stores, but more upscale restaurants have found it hard to attract singles because of a continued stigma about dining alone. "We only get a few single customers each day," said Ms Wang, the waitress. Shanghai singleton Chen Nie, 23, experienced a gamut of emotions when offered a teddy bear at Haidilao. "I was shocked at first. Then I felt warm," she said. "But in the end I felt awkward because it reminded me of the fact that I'm single."

21. Instinct or Cleverness?

We have been brought up to fear insects. We regard them as unnecessary creatures that do more harm than good. We continually wage war on them, for they contaminate our food, carry diseases, or devour our crops. They sting or bite without provocation; they fly uninvited into our rooms on summer nights, or beat against our lighted windows. We live in dread not only of unpleasant insects like spiders or wasps, but of quite harmless one like moths.

Reading about them increases our understanding without dispelling our fears. Knowing that the industrious ant lives in a highly organized society does nothing to prevent us from being filled with revulsion when we find hordes of them crawling over a carefully prepared picnic lunch. No matter how much we like honey, or how much we have read about the uncanny sense of direction which bees possess, we have a horror of being stung. Most of our fears are unreasonable, but they are impossible to erase.

At the same time, however, insects are strangely fascinating. We enjoy reading about them, especially when we find that, like the praying mantis, they lead perfectly horrible lives. We enjoy staring at them, entranced as they go about their business, unaware (we hope) of our presence. Who has not stood in awe at the sight of a spider pouncing on a fly, or a column of ants triumphantly bearing home an enormous dead beetle?

Last summer I spent days in the garden watching thousands of ants crawling up the trunk of my prize peach tree. The tree has grown against a warm wall on a sheltered side of the house. I am especially proud of it, not only because it has survived several severe winters, but because it occasionally produces luscious peaches. During the summer, I noticed that the leaves of the tree were beginning to wither.

Clusters of tiny insects called aphids were to be found on the underside of the leaves. They were visited by a large colony of ants which obtained a sort of honey from them.

I immediately embarked on an experiment which, even though it failed to get rid of the ants, kept me fascinated for twenty-four hours. I bound the base of the tree with sticky tape, making it impossible for the ants to reach the aphids. The tape was so sticky that they did not dare to cross it. For a long time, I watched them scurrying around the base of the tree in bewilderment. I even went out at midnight with a torch and noted with satisfaction (and surprise) that the ants were still swarming around the sticky tape without being able to do anything about it.

I got up early next morning hoping to find that the ants had given up in despair. Instead, I saw that they had discovered a new route. They were climbing up the wall of the house and then on to the leaves of the tree. I realized sadly that I had been completely defeated by their ingenuity. The ants had been quick to find an answer to my thoroughly unscientific methods!

22. A Brief History of Time (Abstract)

A well-known scientist (some say it was Bertrand Russell) once gave a public lecture on astronomy. He described how the earth orbits around the sun and how the sun, in turn, orbits around the center of a vast collection of stars called our galaxy. At the end of the lecture, a little old lady at the back of the room got up and said, "What you have told us is rubbish. The world is really a flat plate supported on the back of a giant tortoise." The scientist gave a superior smile before replying, "What is the tortoise standing on?" "You're very clever, young man, very clever," said the old lady. "But it's turtles all the way down!"

Most people would find the picture of our universe as an infinite tower of tortoises rather ridiculous, but why do we think we know better? What do we know about the universe, and how do we know it? Where did the universe come from, and where is it going? Did the universe have a beginning, and if so, what happened before then? What is the nature of time? Will it ever come to an end? Can we go back in time? Recent breakthroughs in physics, made possible in part by fantastic new technologies, suggest answers to some of these longstanding questions. Someday these answers may seem as obvious to us as the earth orbiting the sun—or perhaps as ridiculous as a tower of tortoises. Only time (whatever that may be) will tell.

23. The Future Vehicle Design

The automotive marketplace will become increasingly fragmented. New vehicle configurations will spawn new vehicle categories to meet a growing number of customer needs. "Crossover" vehicles are the next big wave. These products combine, in varying degrees, the attributes of passenger cars, vans and sport utility vehicles.

Customers will be looking for more diversity, mobility and functionality. Lifestyles will continue to dictate vehicle content. Customers will see a constant stream of innovative products that meet their mobility needs in new and enhanced ways. In addition, functionality will be enhanced through clever ways to access and reconfigure passenger and cargo space.

Vehicle interiors will be more important. Increased passenger time in vehicles will lead to additional comfort and convenience expectations. Ease of entry and exit and improved visibility will have an increasing influence on designs. Concept vehicles will have greater influence. Concepts will increasingly reflect consumer needs, enabling us to move more quickly from concept to production vehicle in response to ever-changing market tastes.

Vehicles will continue to get environmentally cleaner, more fuel-efficient and safer.

24. The Beatles

Even if the word "pop" disappears from the English vocabulary, the influence of pop will remain. Pop has become part of British—and American—history.

There has always been a close cultural link, or tie, between Britain and English-speaking America, not only in literature but also in the popular arts, especially music. Before the Second World War the Americans exported jazz and the blues. During the 1950s they exported rock'n' roll, and star singers like Elvis Presley were idolized by young Britons and Americans alike.

The people responsible for the pop revolution were four Liverpool boys who joined together in a group and called themselves the Beatles. They played in small clubs in the back streets of the city. Unlike the famous solo stars who had their songs written for them, the Beatles wrote their own words and music. They had a close personal relationship with their audience, and they expected them to join in and dance to the "beat" of the music. Audience participation is an essential characteristic of pop culture.

Some pop groups, in particular the Rolling Stones, did more than just entertain. They wrote words which were deliberately intended to shock. They represented the anger and bitterness of youth struggling for freedom against authority, and for this reason they were regarded by some people as the personification of the "permissive society."

The Beatles, on the other hand, finally won the affection — and admiration — of people of all ages and social backgrounds. As they developed, their songs became more serious. They wrote not only of love, but of death and old age and poverty and daily life. They were respected by many intellectuals and by some serious musicians. Largely thanks to the Beatles, pop music has grown into an immense and profitable industry.

25. China's Sports Wear Contest

Li-Ning has two key advantages in reaching the all-important youth market: its products are about half as expensive as those of its foreign rivals, and its network of stores dwarfs that of any other player. To date, though, Li-Ning has been most successful in smaller cities and towns. To really take on the foreign brands, it needs to make a renewed push into the likes of Beijing, Shanghai, and Guangzhou. "Li-Ning is using the Mao Zedong strategy to build expertise in second and third-tier cities," says an industry veteran, "now they have to gain footholds in China's biggest cities."

A looming challenge for all the market leaders is likely to be fast-developing Chinese upstarts. Many of these companies have, until recently, made shoes on contract for the market leaders. And while the vast majority still makes low-quality shoes and clothing, a handful are coming on strong. Anta, based in Fujian Province, and Qingdao-based Double Star both outsell Nike, Adidas, and Li-Ning in volume, though their prices are a fraction of what the leaders charge. Anta is also sponsoring the China Basketball Association, for the second year running, which will raise its profile.

For now, these brands aren't close to competing directly with the top dogs in the market... which leaves Li-Ning to carry the Chinese banner in the competition for shoe domination. "Li-Ning is a very competitive, very powerful brand," says Shen Min, a

Beijing market researcher. "We think it already is as competitive as Nike and Adidas in China." Back on Wangfujing Street, on a gusty winter day, 18-year-old Wu Dizhou would agree. Skipping the Nike and Adidas outlets, Wu rushed for Li-Ning, where he drops $45 on a heavy jacket and a sweatshirt and says he'll return soon for a pair of basketball shoes. "Li-Ning should spend more on advertising so the whole world can know about this high-quality brand," says the student. You can be sure Li-Ning... as well as the other combatants in the Chinese shoe wars... won't disappoint him.

附录二

英译汉篇章练习答案

1. 华盛顿致军队出征演讲

眼前这一刻很可能会决定美国人或成为自由人，或沦为奴隶；他们是否拥有自己的财产；他们的房屋和农场是否会遭受掠夺和摧毁，使他们沦落至悲惨而又无人拯救的境地。美国的数万后代的命运将在上帝的恩赐下，交付于我们这支军队的果敢与信心。残暴冷酷的敌人仅仅留给我们一种选择，要么英勇抗击，要么卑膝投降。因此，我们决心战斗下去。不战斗，毋宁死。

国家和个人的荣誉召唤我们热血男儿拼死疆场；如果我们蒙羞失败，将会声名狼藉，为世人所不齿。就让这掌控着胜利的上帝激励和鼓舞我们去付诸这些伟大而正义的行动吧！让父老乡亲注视的目光带给我们祝福和赞誉，使我们能幸运地挽救他们于水深火热之中。让我们互相激励和鼓舞，告诉整个世界为在自己的土地上赢得自由而奋斗的人们胜过任何卑躬屈膝的雇佣军。

自由、财产、生命和荣誉处在生死存亡的关头。我们流血和备受欺辱的国家的希望取决于你们的英勇奋战；我们的妻儿老小唯一的期待就是我们能给他们带来的太平生活；他们有理由相信上帝会用胜利来酬报我们正义的事业。敌人穷兵黩武地对我们加以威胁，但须记住，他们在各种场合都被勇敢的美国人击溃。他们的战争是罪恶的——他们已经意识到了这一点；如果我们从开始就坚决抵抗，沉着应战，凭借着天时地利，必定会取胜。每个优秀的战士都要严阵以待——保存实力，等候命令，一旦出击，就必定获胜。

2. 致儿子的信

你要学会坦诚待人。坦诚来自诚实和勇气。无论在哪种场合，你都要讲真话并诚心去做正确的事。如果朋友请求帮助且入情入理你应应允；否则的话，坦白告诉他缘由。任何模棱两可的话语都会使他误解，且使自己蒙冤。

不要为了结交朋友或留住友情而做错事；让你这样做的人不值得为之付出如此的代价。与同学和睦相处，建立稳定的关系；你会发现这是经久不衰的准则。尤为重要的是，要以真实面目示人。

如果你发现别人的错误，直接告诉他，不要向其他人抱怨；当面一套，背地一套，没有什么是比这更危险的了。我们的言谈举止，一举一动不应伤害他人。事实上这不仅是处世的最佳原则，而且是赢得安宁与尊敬的最好方式。

关于责任，让我匆忙地在此信结尾时提醒你，大约在一百年前有个异常阴郁、黑暗的一天，称为"黑暗之日"。在这一天，阳光如经历日食般慢慢消失。

责任是我们语言中最崇高的词汇。你诸事要如以前的清教徒一般忠于职守。即使不能多做，也不要期待少做。不要让父母因为你的玩忽职守而平添忧愁。

3. 为什么女人比男人活得长

如果你能拍一张巨幅的集体快照，把今日美国所有的人都容纳进去，就可以看出其中女性比男性多出 600 万人。在这个国家，女人比男人约多活 7 年。当今世界各国，尽管文化不同、饮食不同、生活方式和死亡原因各有不同，有一点则是相同的——女人都比男人活得长。

这要从出生前说起。在妊娠期，男性胎儿多于女性胎儿，约为 110：100。在婴儿出生时，男女之比就已降至约 105：100。人到 30 岁，比数减到男女相当。此后，女人开始领先。80 岁后，女人几乎多出男人一倍。

加州大学圣地亚哥分校的一位流行病学专家德博拉温格德说："不妨查查最前头的 10 种或 12 种死因，每一种都是男人死得多。"她一口气道出种种可悲的结局——心脏病、肺癌、凶杀、肝硬化、肺炎。死于各种结局的男人大致是女人的两倍。

一个世纪以前，美国男人的数量和寿命还都超过女人。但从 20 世纪开始，女性寿命开始增加，这主要是因为怀孕与分娩的危险性降低了。这种差距一直在扩大。到 1946 年，美国的女性人数首次超过了男性。

4. 人一天最重要的 40 分钟，你用好了吗？

我的老师告诉我们这些学生，人在一天之中有 40 分钟记忆力最强，接收能力超过其余 23 小时 20 分钟。而这"记忆超强"的 40 分钟又可以分为两段：临睡前的 20 分钟和醒来后的 20 分钟。

要证明这一理论十分简单。首先，在进入梦乡前把信息植入脑海比在白天乱哄哄的情景下更容易扎根；其次，早晨醒来精力不容易分散，就像空白的页岩，吸收能力更强。这个办法真的很管用，但和其他很多事一样，也需要练习和自律才能日臻完美。

随着语言学习的深入，这个方法不仅对背单词有帮助，也可以成为锻炼听力的最佳时段，而且不论收听的是背景音、晦涩的内容、外语听力材料、广播、电视，还是其他什么。

记忆力除了上学必需外，在各行各业中也很重要。你听过几个演讲人会照本宣科，又见过几个人在做演示时会逐字逐句地朗读每张幻灯片的文字？这样的沟通方式令人厌烦、精力涣散、枯燥乏味、效率低下，保证会让听众兴趣索然、味同嚼蜡，根本就无法说服或激励听众采取行动。但仍有很多人会犯这样的错误。

运用"40分钟"技巧，也许你并不能一字不落地背诵演示稿，却可以充分掌握内容，从而留出更多时间与听众进行眼神交流。你可以让观众参与其中，抽空儿再扫一眼屏幕，不用紧盯不放。你还可以解放胳膊和双手，增加一些动作，以示强调。

5. 朝鲜核问题

联合国安理会成员国正在考虑对朝鲜实施新的制裁，作为对该国第六次，同时也是最强烈的一次核试验的回应。

然而专家表示，中国的支持对增加朝鲜领导人金正恩政府的压力至关重要。

中国外交部长王毅周四表示："联合国安理会应该做出进一步回应，并且采取必要的措施。"

但是王毅表示，"制裁施压"必须与"对话谈判"并重。中国方面表示，加大制裁力度无法缓解朝鲜半岛的紧张局势。

美国总统川普周三与中国国家主席习近平进行了对话。川普称，习主席赞同有必要对朝鲜的核试验做出回应。川普说："他也不想看到朝鲜发生这样的事情。"

美国驻联合国大使尼基·哈利周一表示，安理会15个成员国将会议定一项对朝鲜实施新制裁的决议。她说美国寻求在下周一之前投票表决。

8月5日，联合国安理会通过了第2371号决议，这是对朝鲜7月份进行两次远程导弹试验做出的回应。联合国安理会禁止朝鲜出口煤炭、铁、铅和海鲜产品，附带还有其他限制。这些措施旨在将朝鲜30亿美元的出口收入削减三分之一。

然而，现在有人呼吁削减朝鲜的燃料进口，以对其领导人施加压力。

6. 怀疑自己？

无休止的自我怀疑通常会带来沮丧和焦虑，甚至会导致抑郁症。在《综合精神病学》杂志最近针对107名病人开展的一项研究中，蒙特利尔犹太总医院的戴维·M·敦克利及其同事发现，那些有自我批评倾向的人在四年后最容易产生抑郁症及人际交往障碍，即便他们一开始时并不抑郁。

自我批评也是导致进食失调、自残、躯体变形障碍症——想象自己的身体有缺陷——的因素。纽约美国认知疗法协会会长、精神病专家罗伯特·L·利亚说："我们对于物质成功及外貌的期望不断膨胀，已经变得完全不切实际了。"

很多人在幼年时期便有了自我批评的倾向，之后这个声音便常伴他们左右，成了他们性格的一个部分。心理学家称，儿童，尤其是那些有抑郁倾向遗传的儿童，可能会自己承担并夸大父母、同辈或社会对自己的期望。有一个理论认为，自我批评其实就是冲自身发泄怒气，这类人内心充满了敌对情绪，但是太过忧虑、太没有安全感，不敢把这种情绪发泄出来。其他一些理论则认为，那些责备自己的人是在表达自己的负罪感或羞辱感，或者是下意识里保护自己免遭他人的责备：你不能再来责备我了，我自己已经责备过自己了，用的词比你还要严厉呢。

7. 发展中国家的初级医疗

如今，贫穷国家的人们比过去更长寿也更健康。自 2000 年起，儿童死亡率下降近 50%。新增艾滋病人数的比率下降了 40%。死于疟疾的人数减少了 700 万人。

然而，要做的还有很多。初级护理是医疗卫生最基本的形式，应该是任何完善的医疗体系的核心组成部分。世界卫生组织的一项调查显示，如今有 4 亿人口仍无法享有初级护理。实际人数可能会更多。即使能看全科医师，或更为常见的未完全受过培训的医生或江湖郎中，他们接受的治疗也通常很糟糕。

随着贫穷国家的疾病负担逐渐从传染性疾病转为慢性病，与发达国家趋同，初级护理的糟糕情况将会产生更大的影响。到 2020 年，发展中国家非传染性疾病引起的死亡将占总死亡数的 70%。但大多数高血压、糖尿病或抑郁症患者都无法获得有效治疗，甚至可能都不知道自己生病了。他们应该得到更好的治疗。

初级卫生保健虽不起眼，但确实有效。它就像国家卫生服务的中枢神经系统，监控着社区的总体健康状况，能够治疗慢性疾病以及缓解日常病情，确保传染病不会大规模流行传播。2014 年埃博拉病毒爆发之前，将近一半的利比里亚人负担不起初级护理，致死病毒得以迅速传播开来。在西非部分地区，因其有较完善的初级护理，更轻易地控制了病毒的传播。

8. 机器时代

在一篇名为《成功在美国》的文章中，作者亚当·戴维森讲述了这样一个源自棉花出产国的笑话，笑话是关于现代纺织作坊已高度自动化的事情：现如今，一家普通作坊里只有两名员工，"一个人和一条狗，人在作坊里是为了喂狗，狗在作坊里是为了使人远离机器"。

最近出现了很多类似戴维森所写的文章的文章，它们都表明了这样一种看法：之所以失业人数居高难下和中产阶级收入持续下降，其原因是全球化与信息技术革命已经取得了诸多进步，它们使机器和国外员工在取代本国劳动力方面比以往任何时候都要迅速。

以往，具有一般技术、从事一般工作的员工可以赚得普通的生活。但现如今，普通人才正式地过时了。继续普通无法再让你过上以前的生活，其原因是当下更多的雇主可以用比普通还要低廉的价格，来雇用国外员工，购买机器人和软件，实现自动化，获得天才。因此，每个人都需要挖掘身上额外的东西来让他们做出独特的、有价值的贡献，这种贡献会让他们脱颖而出，不管他们身处什么工作领域。

确实，新科技在过去、现在和将来都在"吞噬"工作岗位，而且这种"吞噬"速度已经提高了，正如戴维森所指出的："（美国）工厂裁员速度是如此之快，以至于在1999—2009年裁员人数超过了之前70年新增员工人数的总和；大约有1/3的制造业工作岗位——总约600万个——消失了。"

9. 青春期

青春期，也就是童年与成年之间的这段时期，可长可短。其长短取决于社会期望值和社会对成熟和成年的定义。在原始社会中，青春期通常是相当短的一段时期。而在工业化社会里，由于人们接受教育时间的延长以及反童工法的制定，青春期要长很多，它包含了人生中第二个十年（10~20岁）的大部分时间。另外，在某一社会中，青春期的长度和成年地位的定义可能会随社会经济条件的改变而改变。这种变化譬如：19世纪后期，美国乃至所有由农业化走向工业化的国家里不再存在青春期和成年期的界限。

现代社会中，青春期的各种仪式已不被正式认可，也不再具有象征意义，人们对其"开始仪式"也不再有统一的认识。社会仪式已经被一系列的"阶段"所取代，这些"阶段"将使人得到更多的认可和更高的社会地位。例如，小学毕业、中学毕业、大学毕业就形成了这样一个系列。每一个"阶段"都意味着某些行为变化和一定的社会认可度，其意义大小则取决于个人的社会经济地位和受教育的目标。青春期的各种仪式也已经被法律意义上的地位、权利、特权和责任所取代。

10. 智能垃圾桶

一款新型"智能垃圾桶"即将问世，有环保意识的家庭再也不用花几个小时把锡罐子、外卖盒、瓶子和纸板箱等垃圾进行分类了。智能垃圾桶可以自动把垃圾按照回收类目进行分类。目前这项发明正在波兰进行试运营，预计几年内就会进入英国市场。这款垃圾桶是由一家名为 Bin.E 的初创公司设计的。垃圾桶的内置系统可以运用传感器、图形识别和人工智能等科技来辨别不同类型的垃圾。当垃圾被倒入后，摄像头和传感器就能识别垃圾的类型，把垃圾放进相应的小垃圾桶，然后可将垃圾进行压缩以减少其所占空间。这款垃圾桶发布之前，曾有报道称因议会希望当地家庭能更多地回收垃圾，有超过100万个家庭的垃圾每隔3~4周才收集处理一次。《每日电讯报》收集的数据显示，至少18个地区已经实行或即将实行每三周收集一次垃圾，3个地区甚至已经在实行或试验每四周收集一次垃圾。虽然普通垃圾收集的次数减少了，但各地方议会增加了回收再利用垃圾的收集次数，力求改变居民的环保习惯。

据传，约翰·路易斯等百货公司正在考虑使用这款垃圾桶。约翰·路易斯曾透露正在引进一款新型的高科技回收垃圾桶，以满足日益增长的消费需求。约翰·路易斯家用设施采购员马特·托马斯说："在短短几个月里，我们的回收专用垃圾桶的销量就大幅增长了25%。我们发现，顾客们越来越注重可持续发展了，他们都会选择双格回收垃圾桶，以便回收各种垃圾。"

11. 读书

过去十年里，儿童文学书籍的销量有了两位数的增长，比图书销量整体增长更快。自2005年以来，儿童书籍的数量翻了三倍多。这在一定程度上反映了针对万千宠爱于一身的独生子女不断增长的产品需求。推动这种需求的原因正是具有成本意识的人们不愿意养更多的子女，而这种意识是独生子女政策所强化的，但是这个政策目前有所松懈。父母越富裕，就越愿意在儿童书籍上花钱。

书商由此看到了一个巨大的赚钱机会。现在大部分成人读物出版商也开始出版儿童读物。去年前100部畅销书中大约有一半是针对儿童的——无论英国还是美国，都没有这么高的比例。而且体裁种类越来越多。为五岁以下儿童量身定做的图画书大受欢迎；针对青少年的小说也在蓬勃发展。

鉴于中国非常重视通过考试，很多书目仅限于传授事实，这一点毫不奇怪。即使孩子还只是在咿呀学语的阶段，家长也会喜欢买非小说类的读物。一些印刷在纸板上、适于两岁及以下儿童的读物竟然旨在教那些婴儿罗马字母表。那些标题为"如何成为气象学家"或是"科学巨星"等系列儿童读物销量都很不错。

12. 中国能源

能源是人类社会赖以生存和发展的重要物质基础。纵观人类社会发展的历史，人类文明的每一次重大进步都伴随着能源的改进和更替。能源的开发利用极大地推进了世界经济和人类社会的发展。过去100多年里，发达国家先后完成了工业化，消耗了地球上大量的自然资源，特别是能源资源。当前，一些发展中国家正在步入工业化阶段，能源消费增加是经济和社会发展的客观必然。

中国是当今世界上最大的发展中国家，发展经济、摆脱贫困，是中国政府和中国人民在相当长一段时期内的主要任务。20世纪70年代末以来，中国作为世界上发展最快的发展中国家，经济社会发展取得了举世瞩目的辉煌成就，成功地开辟了中国特色社会主义道路，为世界的发展和繁荣做出了重大贡献。

中国是目前世界上第二位能源生产国和消费国。能源供应持续增长，为经济社会发展提供了重要的支撑。能源消费的快速增长，为世界能源市场创造了广阔的发展空间。中国已经成为世界能源市场不可或缺的重要组成部分，对维护全球能源安全正在发挥着越来越重要的积极作用。

13. 悲剧神话

谁没有体验过这种情况——既不得不看，又同时向往视野之外的东西，谁就很难想象，在欣赏悲剧神话之际，这两种过程明明是同时并存同时感受的。真正的审美观众会证实我的话；我认为，在悲剧的特殊效果中，只有这种并存现象最值得注意。现在，如果把观众的审美现象转化为悲剧艺术家的审美过程，您就不难明白悲剧神话的起源了。悲剧神话，具有梦境艺术那种对假象和静观的快感，但同时又否定这种快感，并在这鲜明的假象世界之毁灭中得到更高的满足。

悲剧神话的内容，首先是歌颂战斗英雄的史诗事件。然而，英雄的厄运、极惨淡的胜利、极痛苦的动机冲突，简言之，西烈诺斯智慧之明证，或者用美学术语来说，丑恶与和谐，往往再三出现在许多民间文学形式中——尤其是在一个民族精力充沛的幼年时代。这种莫明其妙的特点从何而来呢？难道人们对这些东西真的具有更高的快感吗？

14. 帕斯特斯基

被比作史蒂芬·霍金以及阿尔伯特·爱因斯坦这样的天才这种事不会发

生在一个普通人身上。所以当我们告诉你萨布丽娜·冈萨雷斯·帕斯特斯基远远超过了普通人的水准，我们是认真的。

年仅 23 岁的帕斯特斯基所取得的成就已经超过了我们多数人一生才能获得的成绩。在她只有 14 岁的时候，这位芝加哥少女就独自建造了自己的单发动机飞机。如果这还不够让人印象深刻的话，之后她又驾驶着飞机飞越了密歇根湖，成为有史以来最年轻的驾驶着自己的飞机航行的人。整场冒险活动用了两年才完成，而且她还记录了自己的所有经历并上传到了 YouTube 上。之后，在 2010 年她从伊利诺伊数理高中毕业，然后进入著名的麻省理工学院。她在麻省理工学院只用了三年时间就取得了最高的平均绩点 5.0。如今她在举世闻名的哈佛大学攻读博士学位，拥有完全的学术自由，并且不会受到工作人员的干扰。

再说一次，她只有 23 岁。更非凡的是，如今她不再对造飞机感兴趣了，而是把注意力放在了物理学上，例如黑洞理论以及重力是如何影响空间和时间的，因此我们把她比作了爱因斯坦和霍金。她特别想研究"量子引力"，想试着了解重力与量子物理学之间的关系。如果她的研究成功的话，在这一领域的发现会极大地改变我们了解宇宙的方式。在今年早些时候的一次采访中，她说："你要对你相信自己能做到的事持乐观态度。在你小的时候，你讲了许多关于自己将来要做什么或是长大后要成为什么样的人，我认为重要的是不要忘记曾经的梦想。"

15. 科比·布莱恩特

我记得对阵科比的最艰难的一场发生在波士顿，我想他已经在我面前连续命中 7~8 个投篮。所以我们叫了一个暂停围在一块，教练看着我的表情我能理解，他想让我限制住科比，球队的其余队员知道发生了什么，他们也用同样的表情看着我。最后他们提出或许我们应该用车轮战来对付他，当时我大喊道："天哪，不，我来防他，我自己能搞定。"

在我的防守下，那场比赛的最后九次投篮他都投丢了，然后我们赢了。但是那场比赛的数据统计仍然历历在目，科比投了 47 个篮，47 个，从来没有哪个人在我面前投过 47 个，要知道一支球队的大多数投篮次数只有 81~89 次。

你必须知道科比在一场比赛出手如此多次意味着什么，他一丝不苟地消耗防守者，直到他们彻底崩溃。他的整个职业生涯就是即使让防守者失去信心也在不停地攻击他们。要知道，他靠这一点赢得了五个总冠军。

如果你想成功地防住科比，那么你不能崩溃。说起来容易做起来难呀！

16. 以书为伴

通常看一个人读些什么书就可知道他的为人，就像看他同什么人交往就可知道他的为人一样，因为有人以人为伴，也有人以书为伴。无论是书友还是朋友，我们都应该以最好的为伴。

好书就像是你最好的朋友。它始终不渝，过去如此，现在如此，将来也永远不变。它是最有耐心、最令人愉悦的伴侣。在我们穷愁潦倒、临危遭难时，它也不会抛弃我们，对我们总是一如既往的亲切。在我们年轻时，好书陶冶我们的性情，增长我们的知识；到我们年老时，它又给我们以慰藉和勉励。

人们常常因为喜欢同一本书而结为知己，就像有时两个人因为敬慕同一个人而成为朋友一样。有句古谚说道："爱屋及乌。"其实"爱我及书"这句话蕴涵更多的哲理。书是更为真诚而高尚的情谊纽带。人们可以通过共同喜爱的作家沟通思想、交流感情，彼此息息相通，并与自己喜欢的作家思想相通、情感相融。

好书常如最精美的宝器，珍藏着人生的思想的精华，因为人生的境界主要就在于其思想的境界。因此，最好的书是金玉良言和崇高思想的宝库，这些良言和思想若铭记于心并多加珍视，就会成为我们忠实的伴侣和永恒的慰藉。

书籍具有不朽的本质，是为人类努力创造的最为持久的成果。寺庙会倒塌，神像会朽烂，而书却经久长存。对于伟大的思想来说，时间是无关紧要的。多年前初次闪现于作者脑海的伟大思想今日依然清新如故。时间唯一的作用是淘汰不好的作品，因为只有真正的佳作才能经世长存。

书籍介绍我们与最优秀的人为伍，使我们置身于历代伟人巨匠之间，如闻其声，如观其行，如见其人，同他们情感交融，悲喜与共，感同身受。我们觉得自己仿佛在作者所描绘的舞台上和他们一起粉墨登场。

即使在人世间，伟大杰出的人物也让人永生不忘。他们的精神被载入书册，传于四海。书是人生至今仍在聆听的智慧之声，永远充满着活力。

17. 人性

高级动物会参与个体斗争，但是不会参加有组织的、大规模的屠杀，人是唯一一个热衷参加战争这最残暴活动的动物，人是唯一的那种将同胞聚集起来发动血腥战争并冷静镇压同类的动物，人是唯一的那种为了肮脏的军饷就去征战的动物，就像黑森在独立战争中做得那样，帮助杀戮同类的陌生人，这些人没有做过伤害他的事情，也没有与他有任何争执。

人是唯一的抢夺绝望无助同类国土的动物，抢夺他们的财产，驱逐他们，摧毁他们。人从古至今都这么做，地球上没有一块土地有它公正合法的拥有者，没有一块土地不是通过武力杀戮从拥有者手中抢走的。

人是唯一的奴隶，也是唯一奴隶别人的动物，他总是以这样或那样的形式被奴役，也总是以这样或那样的方式奴役别人。在我们的时代，人总是为了工资被奴役，干别人的活，而这个奴隶又奴役比他工资更微薄的奴隶，别人又干他的工作，高级动物是唯一一个干自己的工作而自食其力的动物。

人是唯一的爱国者，他自诩与众不同，打着自己的旗帜，轻视别的国家，不惜重金豢养无数着装统一的杀手，就是为了掠夺别人的土地，阻止别人掠夺自己的土地。在战争期间，他洗净自己双手的鲜血，大肆鼓吹人类的博爱，当然也只是耍嘴皮子而已。

18. 毕业致辞

有人说，雨是天上落下来的彩色纸屑。今天上午下了雨，连老天爷都在和我们一起庆祝今天这场隆重的毕业典礼啊。

在我开始之前，你们有一件很重要的事需要做一下，今天你们的父母和监护人都坐在你们的身后。在两年、三年或者四年以前，他们开车来到卡迪根，送你下车，帮你安顿下来，然后转身离开。这对他们而言是一次很大的牺牲。他们流着泪回到家，家里空间更大却更孤独了。他们这样做，是因为让你们接受教育这个决定关乎着你们的未来。也正是因为他们做出了这样的牺牲，你们才是现在的你们。所以今天的毕业典礼不仅是你们的事儿，也是他们的事儿。我希望你们能够起立，并转身向他们致以掌声。

如果有人问我今天在这里的演讲如何，我就可以说演讲被掌声打断了，哈哈。

恭喜你们，2017届的毕业生。你们已经来到了人生的一个重要的阶段，这里是你们的里程碑。很抱歉，这是你人生中最容易的一个阶段（书里说的）。但是你们现在身处卡迪根中学——这个国际社区的一分子，这一点你们应该意识到。

如今，各个国家的大学、高中、初中的毕业典礼上，毕业生们会听得不耐烦，演讲者基本上总是讲同样的话。他们会说今天的毕业典礼只是一次联系。这只是一次开始，并不是结束，你们应该向前看。这倒是说得很对。

19. 何江的哈佛演讲

尽管人类已经掌握和积累了大量知识，但是我们还是没能很好地把它们运用在最需要的地方。世界银行的数据显示，世界上大约有12%的人口每天的生活水平在2美元以下。每年都会有300万名儿童因营养不良而死亡。全球有3亿人仍然饱受疟疾之苦。在世界各地，我们经常看到贫穷、疾病和资源短缺，这些都阻碍了科学知识的传播。现代社会里那些习以为常的救生知识在不发达地区还未普及。于是，在世界上很多地区，人们仍然用火疗的方法来处理蜘蛛咬伤事件。

在哈佛读书期间，我看到科学知识是如何以一种简约而不简单的方式来帮助他人的。在2000年的时候，禽流感肆虐，对我们村而言，这种病就像是魔鬼的诅咒。村里的土方法也束手无策。另外，村民们弄不清普通感冒和流感的区别，他们并不懂得流感比普通感冒更致命。而且，大部分人根本不了解流感病毒可以在不同的物种之间传播。

所以当我了解了简单有效的卫生措施——比如隔离不同的动物可以遏制疾病的传播，并把这样的信息告诉我的村民的时候，我的心里第一次有了作为未来科学家的成就感和使命感。我还感受到了，它是我个人道德发展的重要转折点，也让我明白了我是地球大家庭中的一员。

哈佛让我们敢于做梦，让我们渴望改变世界。今天在这个毕业典礼上，大家可能正幻想着等待我们的伟大理想和征途。对我而言，我却想着我家乡的那些村民。我的这段经历提醒着我对于一个研究人员，把知识传播给最需要它们的人是多么的重要。因为通过使用我们已经掌握的科学，我们可以把我家乡的村民和成千上万类似的人带入你我熟知的世界。这是我们每一个人都可以发挥的影响！

20. 中国的单身贵族

食客们簇拥在一锅热汤旁，将荤素菜肴放在底料中煮熟，火锅已经被公认为中国美食的精华。但是中国的火锅连锁巨头有了一种新手段去吸引单身食客用餐：毛绒熊。

200家海底捞火锅店用毛绒玩具陪伴单身食客用餐，这凸显了中国人口结构变化已催生出众多单身食客，商家纷纷努力抓住这种变化带来的商机。上海海底捞店的服务生王萍（音）说"他们可以减轻人们的孤独感"，并向《金融时报》透露顾客可以在大泰迪熊和黄色毛绒鸡中任选其一。

据欧睿咨询公司汇编的官方数据显示，2012年以来，中国独自生活的成年人已增多16%，达到7 700万人，且有望在2021年增至9 200万人。中国人的晚婚趋势导致了这种人口变化，这一趋势在繁荣的城市尤为突出。在上海，女性首婚平均年龄从2011年的27岁增至30岁。由于过去十年中国的离婚率增加了一倍,所以婚姻持续的时间也相对减少。波士顿咨询集团的数据显示,如今中国16%的城市人口独自一人生活。

波士顿集团在最近的报告中说:"这种趋势还伴随着人们对于保持单身的观念的巨大改变,单身观念不再受鄙夷。"这也意味着单身人士会"自己就餐、自己旅游、自己从事各种活动"。商家们也已经对这种已在东亚邻国日本和韩国出现的人口变化趋势做出反应。日本连锁店无印良品专为中国单身人士推出更小的电饭煲、烤箱和水壶。阿里巴巴将每年的十一月十一日定为双十一购物节,来庆祝单身生活,现已成为一年一度的消费盛宴,去年单日销售额高达1 207亿元人民币。

英敏特咨询公司近期报道显示,当被问及最喜欢如何度过闲暇时光时,中国的单身人士选择在线看电影或者旅行,"使其简单平凡的生活更让人兴奋"。报告补充道,与已婚人士相比,他们不太可能会和家人一起"走亲戚"或者购物,而更喜欢观光和体验当地的文化。

食品外卖行业也受益于这种单身趋势。贝恩公司的数据显示,去年中国食品外卖行业销售额增长44%。中国最大的外卖服务业饿了么,今年上半年销售额增加了127%,其发言人杨耿申(音)说:"以我的经验来说,很少一部分的单身人士会自己做饭。"

美团点评是一家餐厅点评和提供食品外卖服务的公司,该公司表示其订单中65%来自未婚人士,其中快餐是单身人士最喜欢订购的食物。"单身人士对于我们来说是最重要的消费人群",美团外卖经理王莆中说道。他还补充说:"中式菜肴做起来十分复杂……需要耗费大量时间,所以单身人士认为,订外卖要方便得多。"

在快餐店和便利店中,单身食客随处可见,但相对高档的餐厅很难见到他们的身影,因为一个人吃饭仍会受到异样的眼光。服务生王女士说:"我们一天仅有几个单身顾客来用餐。"上海的一名23岁单身人士陈聂(音),在吃海底捞时身旁有一只泰迪熊陪着她,但是她的情绪跌宕起伏,"刚开始我很吃惊,随后我感觉很温暖,"她说。"但是最后我觉得很尴尬,因为这提醒着我实际上我是一个单身人。"

21. 是本能还是机智?

我们自幼就在对昆虫的惧怕中长大。我们把昆虫当作害多益少的无用东西。人类不断同昆虫斗争,因为昆虫弄脏我们的食物、传播疾病、吞噬庄稼。它们无缘无故地又叮又咬;夏天的晚上,它们未经邀请便飞到我们房间里,或者对着露出亮光的窗户乱扑乱撞。我们在日常生活中,不但憎恶如蜘蛛、黄蜂之类令人讨厌的昆虫，而且憎恶并无大害的飞蛾等。

阅读有关昆虫的书能增加我们对它们的了解，却不能消除我们恐惧的心理。即使知道勤奋的蚂蚁生活在具有高度组织性的社会里，当看到大群蚂蚁在我们精心准备的午间野餐上爬行时，我们也无法抑制对它们的反感。不管我们多么爱吃蜂蜜，或读过多少关于蜜蜂具有神秘的识别方向的灵感的书，我们仍然十分害怕被蜂蜇。我们的恐惧大部分是没有道理的，但无法消除。

同时，不知为什么昆虫又是迷人的。我们喜欢看有关昆虫的书，尤其是当我们了解螳螂等过着一种令人生畏的生活时，就更加爱读有关昆虫的书了。我们喜欢入迷地看它们做事，它们不知道（但愿如此）我们就在它们身边。当看到蜘蛛扑向一只苍蝇时，一队蚂蚁抬着一只巨大的死甲虫凯旋时，谁能不感到敬畏呢？

去年夏天，我花了好几天时间站在花园里观察成千只蚂蚁爬上我那棵心爱的桃树的树干。那棵树是靠着房子有遮挡的一面暖墙生长的。我为这棵树感到特别自豪，不仅因为它度过了几个寒冬终于活了下来，还因为它有时结出些甘甜的桃子来。到了夏天，我发现树叶开始枯萎，结果在树叶背面找到成串的叫作蚜虫的小虫子。蚜虫遭到一窝蚂蚁的攻击，蚂蚁从它们身上可以获得一种蜜。

我当即动手做了一项试验，这项试验尽管没有使我摆脱这些蚂蚁，却使我着迷了24小时。我用一条胶带把桃树底部包上，不让蚂蚁接近蚜虫。胶带极黏，蚂蚁不敢从上面爬过。在很长一段时间里，我看见蚂蚁围着大树底部来回转悠，不知所措。半夜，我还拿着电筒来到花园里，满意地（同时惊奇地）发现那些蚂蚁还围着胶带团团转。无能为力。

第二天早上，我起床后希望看见蚂蚁已因无望而放弃了尝试，结果却发现它们又找到一条新的路径。它们正在顺着房子的外墙往上爬，然后爬上树叶。我懊丧地感到败在了足智多谋的蚂蚁的手下。蚂蚁已很快找到了相应的对策，来对付我那套完全不科学的办法！

22. 时间简史（摘录）

一位著名的科学家（据说是贝特朗·罗素）曾经作过一次关于天文学方面的讲演。他描述了地球如何绕着太阳运动，以及太阳又是如何绕着我们称为星系的巨大的恒星群的中心转动。演讲结束之时，一位坐在房间后排的矮个老妇人站起来说道："你说的这些都是废话。这个世界实际上是驮在一只大乌龟的背上的一块平板。"这位科学家很有教养地微笑着答道："那么这只乌龟是站在什么上面的呢？""你很聪明，年轻人，的确很聪明，"老妇人说，

"不过，这是一只驮着一只一直驮下去的乌龟群啊！"

大部分人会觉得，把我们的宇宙喻为一个无限的乌龟塔相当荒谬，可是为什么我们自以为知道得更多一些呢？我们对宇宙了解了多少？而我们又是怎样知道的呢？宇宙从何而来，又将向何处去？宇宙有开端吗？如果有的话，在这开端之前发生了什么？时间的本质是什么？它会有一个终结吗？在物理学上的一些最新突破，使一部分奇妙的新技术得以实现，从而对于回答这些长期以来悬而未决问题中的某些问题有所启发。也许有一天这些答案会像我们认为地球绕着太阳运动那样显而易见——当然也可能像乌龟塔那般荒唐可笑。不管怎样，唯有让时间来判断了。

23. 未来汽车设计

汽车市场将会进一步细分，新车型将会产生新的汽车分类以满足顾客不断增长的多样化需求。"交叉车型"汽车是下一个潮流，这些产品将在不同程度上融合轿车、旅行车和运动型功能车的特性。

顾客将希望看到更多的变化、更好的移动性以及更完善的功能，生活方式将继续决定汽车的内涵。顾客将看到具有创新意义的产品不断涌现，这些产品将以全新的和更好的方式满足他们的移动需求。除此之外，通过更灵活的进入方式和重新布置乘员及货物的空间，汽车的功能将会进一步加强。

汽车的内饰将会更重要；乘员在车内逗留时间的增加，将导致顾客对汽车舒适性和便利性产生更多的期望。方便的上下车和改进的可视性将对汽车设计产生更大的影响。概念车的影响将会更大，将会更多地反映顾客的需求，使得我们能够更为迅捷地将概念车转化为产品以应对永远变化着的市场品位。

今后汽车还将更加清洁、省油和安全。

24. 披头士乐队

即使"流行音乐"这个词从英语词汇中消失，其影响仍将日久天长。流行音乐已经成为英国历史（以及美国历史）的一部分。

英国和说英语的北美国家之间一直在文化上有着密切的联系，这不仅仅表现在文学方面，还表现在通俗艺术方面，尤其是通俗音乐。在第二次世界大战之前，美国人把爵士乐和布鲁斯音乐传播到国外。到了50年代，他们的摇滚乐又在全世界流传开来，像埃尔维斯·普雷斯利这样的歌星成了英国和美国的年轻人崇拜的偶像。

引起一场流行音乐革命的是4个利物浦的小伙子，他们凑在一起自称为披头士乐队，在利物浦穷街陋巷的小夜总会里演唱。一般独唱歌星演唱的歌都是别人专门为他们写的，但披头士乐队却迥然不同，他们自己作词谱曲。他们与观众相互密切沟通，并期望观众也介入进来，跟着音乐的节奏纵情跳舞。观众的参与是通俗文化的一个基本特征。

有些流行乐队，尤其是滚石乐队，不只是为了娱乐才表演，他们创作歌词时就是让人们感到震惊，他们表达了青年人在力求摆脱权威的过程中愤怒和痛苦的心情。正是由于这一原因，有些人把他们看作"放纵的社会"的化身。

而披头士乐队最终却赢得了所有年龄层次和社会各阶层人士的好感与赞赏。随着披头士乐队逐渐成长，他们的歌曲也越来越严肃。他们不仅仅创作爱情歌曲，还描写死亡、老年、贫困和日常生活，因而得到了许多知识界人士和一些严肃音乐家们的钦佩。流行音乐之所以发展成为今天如此庞大和赢利的行业，主要受益于披头士乐队。

25. 中国运动服装市场上的竞争者

李宁公司在攻占至关重要的青少年市场方面有两个主要的优势：一是其产品价格约为其外国竞争者的一半；二是其专营店网络超过任何一个竞争对手。尽管迄今为止，李宁在小城镇中最为成功，但如要迎接国外品牌的挑战，李宁则需要重新挺进北京、上海和广州这一类大城市。"李宁正采用毛泽东的游击战略，在二三级城市建立自己的优势，"一位行业内资深人士说，"现在李宁公司将不得不去几个中国最大城市争取一席之地。"

市场领先品牌所面临的一个隐现的挑战很有可能是中国市场上快速崛起的本土公司。直到最近，很多这类公司还在为领先品牌进行合同代工。虽然这类公司大多数仍然在生产质量低下的鞋子和衣服，极少数公司则在强势发展。总部设在福建的安踏及青岛的双星，其销量均已超过耐克、阿迪达斯和李宁，尽管其价格比领先品牌的价格要低得多。安踏已连续两年赞助中国篮球协会，该项举措将会提升其形象。

这些品牌现在还无法和市场上的领先品牌直接竞争，所以只有李宁公司在争夺鞋类市场王者的竞争中独扛中国大旗。"李宁是一个很有竞争力、十分强大的品牌，"北京的一位名叫沈民（译音）的市场研究员说，"我们认为李宁在中国市场上具有同耐克、阿迪达斯一样的竞争力。"回到王府井，在一个寒风凛冽的冬日，年仅18的学生吴迪州（译音）也同意上述说法。在很快逛完耐克和阿迪达斯的零售店后，他冲向李宁品牌店，在那里他付了45美元买了一件防风上衣和一件汗衫；他说他将很快再次光顾该公司买一双篮球鞋。"李宁公司应该花钱多做些广告，这样全世界才能知道这个高质量的品牌，"他说。你可以相信，李宁以及中国鞋业大战中的其他参与者不会让他失望。

参考文献

[1] Austen, Jane. 1994. *Pride and Prejudice* [M]. Beijing: Foreign Language Teaching and Research Press.

[2] Bassnett, Susan. 2004. *Translation Studies* [M]. Shanghai: Shanghai Foreign Language Education Press.

[3] Dollerup, Cay. 2007. *Basics of Translation Studies* [M]. Shanghai: Shanghai Foreign Language Education Press.

[4] Lefevere, Andre. 2004. *Translation, Rewriting and the Manipulation of Literary Fame* [M]. Shanghai: Shanghai Foreign Language Education Press.

[5] Nida, E. A. 1984. *Approaches to Translating in the Western World* [M]. Beijing: Foreign Language Teaching and Research Press.

[6] Schulte, Rainer & Biguenet, John. 1992. *Theories of Translation: An Anthology of Essays from Dryden to Derrida* [M]. Chicago: The University of Chicago Press.

[7] Steiner, George. 2001. *After Babel: Aspects of Language and Translation* [M]. Shanghai: Shanghai Foreign Language Education Press.

[8] [德] 爱克曼. 歌德谈话录 [M]. 朱光潜, 译. 北京: 人民文学出版社, 1978.

[9] [苏] 巴尔胡达罗夫. 语言与翻译 [M]. 蔡毅, 虞杰, 译. 北京: 中国对外翻译出版公司, 1985.

[10] 蔡薇. 翻译中词义轻重的选择 [J]. 大同职业技术学院学报, 2001 (03): 56-57.

[11] 陈宏薇. 新编汉英翻译教程 [M]. 上海: 上海外语教育出版社, 2004.

[12] 陈淑芳, 张惠玲. 英语翻译中的正反译法 [J]. 商洛师范专科学校学报, 2002 (01): 52-54.

[13] 程洪珍. 东西方传统思维方式与英汉语言差异 [J]. 安徽大学学报, 2005 (03): 50-53.

[14] 董明. 词义空缺与翻译 [J]. 浙江工程学院学报, 1999, 16 (2):

134-138.

[15] 范建华. 浅论英语词义褒贬的选择与翻译 [J]. 江苏教育学院学报（社会科学版），2001（05）：86-87.

[16] 范振辉. 英语特殊状语从句的理解及其翻译 [J]. 湖北广播电视大学学报，2008（11）：101-102.

[17] 范秀英. 价值观念与英汉语言差异 [J]. 外语教学，2005（02）：37-39.

[18] 范仲英. 实用翻译教程 [M]. 北京：外语教学与研究出版社，1994.

[19] 冯庆华，龚芬. 翻译引论 [M]. 北京：高等教育出版社，2011：80.

[20] 冯庆华. 实用翻译教程 [M]. 上海：上海外语教育出版社，2002.

[21] 冯伟年. 新编实用英汉翻译实例评析 [M]. 北京：清华大学出版社，2006.

[22] 高强，李曹. 浅谈直译法与意译法在翻译工作中的应用 [J]. 科技信息（科学教研），2008（14）：263-264.

[23] 葛陈荣，汪浪. 论英语长句、难句汉译的方法 [J]. 内蒙古农业大学学报（社会科学版），2006（01）：280-282.

[24] [德]歌德. 歌德自传 [M]. 上海：上海三联书店，1998.

[25] 耿智，马慧芳. 认知-功能视角下英语定语从句的翻译 [J]. 上海翻译，2015（01）：42-45.

[26] 龚翰熊. 欧洲小说史 [M]. 成都：四川大学出版社，1997.

[27] 韩彩英，武娟娟. 从语法-逻辑构造差别看中西思维差异——以英汉语言比较为例 [J]. 理论月刊，2014（06）：77-80.

[28] 韩小聪. 试析直译、意译在比喻翻译中的应用 [J]. 西昌学院学报（自然科学版），2004（03）：105-107.

[29] 何刚强. 笔译理论与技巧 [M]. 北京：外语教学与研究出版社，2009.

[30] 胡晨飞. "直译""意译"之历史溯源与理论界说 [J]. 英语研究，2009，7（01）：51-56，39.

[31] 胡状麟. 语篇的衔接与连贯 [M]. 上海：上海外语教育出版社，1984.

[32] 黄静. 英汉语言差异在翻译中对意义传译的影响 [J]. 安徽农业大学学报（社会科学版），2008（01）：84-86.

[33] 黄吟. 英美名家历史文化名篇选译 [M]. 北京：北京理工大学出版社，2012.

[34] 黄永亮. When引导的时间状语从句的翻译 [J]. 咸阳师专学报，1997

（04）：43-45.

[35] 黄源深. 英语笔译实务 [M]. 北京：外文出版社，2014.

[36] [英]简·奥斯汀. 傲慢与偏见 [M]. 孙致礼，译. 南京：译林出版社，1993.

[37] 蒋爱萍. 转译法在科技英语中的应用 [J]. 宿州教育学院学报，2003（01）：60-61.

[38] 靳锁，冯超. 减词法在英汉翻译中的应用 [J]. 科教文汇（下旬刊），2008（08）：244.

[39] 柯林斯高阶英汉双解学习词典 [M]. 柯克尔，译. 北京：外语教学与研究出版社，2011.

[40] 李雯. 英汉语言差异引起的常见英汉翻译问题评价 [J]. 山东农业工程学院学报，2016，33（09）：150-152.

[41] 李田心. "直译"和"意译"新解——"直译""意译"与词义相关，与形式无关 [J]. 皖西学院学报，2014，30（06）：87-91，108.

[42] 连淑能. 英汉对比研究 [M]. 北京：高等教育出版社，2016.

[43] 廖七一. 当代西方翻译理论探索 [M]. 南京：译林出版社，2000.

[44] 卢敏. 英语笔译全真试题解析（2级）[M]. 北京：外文出版社，2017.

[45] 卢敏. 英语笔译全真试题解析（3级）[M]. 北京：外文出版社，2017.

[46] 吕银平. "直译与意译，归化与异化"译法之我见 [J]. 宁夏师范学院学报，2007（04）：136-138.

[47] 林基海. 英译汉"反译法"探讨 [J]. 中国翻译，1983（05）：17-19.

[48] 凌渭民. 科技英语翻译中的省译法 [J]. 外国语，1982（01）：37-38.

[49] 刘金龙. 试论科技英语中名词性从句的分类与翻译 [J]. 英语知识，2009（09）：35-38.

[50] 马丙权. 浅谈英译汉中的正反互译法 [J]. 山东外语教学，1989（03）：65-69.

[51] 马秉义. 英译汉教程新编 [M]. 上海：上海交通大学出版社，2015.

[52] 马永峰. 英译汉中句子的切分译法 [J]. 河北理工大学学报（社会科学版），2011，11（03）：152-154.

[53] 毛新耕. 论英汉翻译中的语序调整 [J]. 广西社会科学，2004（04）：122-125.

[54] 马海琴. 浅谈英汉翻译中词义的选择和确定 [J]. 太原经济管理干部学院学报，2004（01）：162-163.

[55] 欧阳燕. 长句的逻辑翻译法 [J]. 西安外国语学院学报, 2005 (02): 78-80.

[56] 潘文国. 当代西方的翻译学研究——兼谈"翻译学"的学科性问题 [J]. 西北工业大学学报, 2002 (3): 32.

[57] 潘文国. 汉英语对比研究纲要 [M]. 北京: 北京语言文化大学出版社, 2002.

[58] 秦洪武, 王克非. 英汉比较与翻译 [M]. 北京: 外语教学与研究出版社, 2010.

[59] 邱懋如. 英译汉词义选择问题浅谈 [J]. 中国翻译, 1983 (04): 16-19.

[60] [法]伏尔泰, 狄德罗, 拉哈勃. 莎士比亚词典 [M]. 朱雯, 张君川, 译. 合肥: 安徽文艺出版社, 1992.

[61] 商颖. 增词法在英汉翻译中的应用 [J]. 长春师范学院学报, 2010, 29 (11): 150-151.

[62] 司显柱, 曾剑平. 英译汉教程 [M]. 北京: 北京大学出版社, 2006.

[63] 孙萍. 论减省译法 [J]. 吉林省经济管理干部学院学报, 2000 (05): 59-61.

[64] 孙迎春. 剩余信息理论与英汉翻译中的增词减词技巧 [J]. 中国翻译, 1988 (04): 16-20.

[65] 孙万彪. 高级翻译教程 [M]. 上海: 上海外语教育出版社, 2000.

[66] 谭载喜. 西方翻译简史 (增订版) [M]. 北京: 商务印书馆, 2004.

[67] 谭载喜. 奈达论翻译 [M]. 北京: 中国对外翻译出版公司, 1984.

[68] 唐述宗. 论英语汉译中的"正反互逆"问题 [J]. 天津外国语学院学报, 1997 (04): 16-20.

[69] 唐志高. 正反译法及其原则 [J]. 海峡科学, 2011 (10): 87, 95.

[70] 倜西, 董乐山. 英汉翻译手册 [M]. 北京: 商务印书馆, 2002.

[71] 王海武. 浅谈名词性从句的翻译 [J]. 和田师范专科学校学报, 2008 (04): 153-154.

[72] 王宏印. 英汉翻译综合教程 [M]. 大连: 辽宁师范大学出版社, 2002.

[73] 王军. 对翻译定义、原则和标准的再思考 [J]. 和田师范专科学校学报, 2007 (02): 128-129.

[74] 王蕾. 英语构词转类法与英汉翻译词汇转译法 [J]. 上海翻译, 2006 (03): 24-27.

[75] 谢天振. 现行翻译定义已落后于时代的发展——对重新定位和定义翻译的几点反思 [J]. 中国翻译, 2015, 36 (03): 14-15.

[76] 谢天振. 当代西方翻译研究的三大突破和两大转向 [J]. 四川外语学院学报, 2003 (5): 110.

[77] 谢天振. 当代国外翻译理论导读 [M]. 天津: 南开大学出版社, 2008.

[78] 熊兵. 翻译标准研究综述 [J]. 高等函授学报（哲学社会科学版）, 2000 (04): 5-7, 36.

[79] 许建平. 英汉互译实践与技巧（第 3 版）[M]. 北京: 清华大学出版社, 2009.

[80] 许兰. 英汉语言对比在文化领域的思考 [J]. 科技信息, 2011 (09): 516, 494.

[81] 许渊冲. 翻译的艺术 [M]. 北京: 五洲传播出版社, 2006.

[82] 杨琦. 英译汉翻译技巧之词类转译法 [J]. 西南科技大学学报（哲学社会科学版）, 2003 (04): 91-93.

[83] 杨士焯. 英汉翻译教程 [M]. 北京: 北京大学出版社, 2011.

[84] 杨秀兰. 浅析英汉翻译过程中词义的选择 [J]. 内蒙古民族大学学报, 2007 (03): 37-39.

[85] 尹富林, 阮玉慧. 英汉互译: 理论与实践 [M]. 合肥: 中国科学技术大学出版社, 2007.

[86] 张培基. 英汉翻译教程 [M]. 上海: 上海外语教育出版社, 2002.

[87] 张韵斐. 现代英语词汇学概论 [M]. 北京: 北京师范大学出版社, 1987.

[88] 张泽乾. 翻译经纬 [M]. 武汉: 武汉大学出版社, 1994.

[89] 章振邦. 新编英语语法教程 [M]. 上海: 上海外语教育出版社, 2009.

[90] 赵红军, 王雪艳. 词类转译法在《傲慢与偏见》汉译本中的运用 [J]. 辽宁工学院学报（社会科学版）, 2000 (02): 86-88.

[91] 赵妍艳. 目的论与英汉翻译技巧之增减词 [J]. 赤峰学院学报（自然科学版）, 2014, 30 (11): 211-212.

[92] 郑昌锭. 论增词法在科技英语翻译中的应用 [J]. 荆州师专学报, 1995 (03): 70-75.

[93] 郑昌锭. 论减词法在科技英语翻译中的应用 [J]. 福建外语, 1997 (03): 51-54.

[94] 郑守志. 英译汉技巧中词类转译法的学习与研究 [J]. 首都医科大学学

报（社会科学版），2010（00）：325-329.

[95] 钟书能. 信息结构——英汉被动句主位强调说质疑 [J]. 外国语，1997（05）：46-52.

[96] 周成. 英汉翻译中的增词法 [J]. 成都大学学报（社会科学版），2006（03）：126-127.

[97] 周成，王慧. 试论定语从句的翻译方法 [J]. 成都大学学报（教育科学版），2008（01）：44-45，51.

[98] 周永霞. 文学作品翻译技巧之增词法的应用 [J]. 文学教育（上），2010（03）：117.

[99] 朱菊芬. 英汉比较与定语从句的翻译 [J]. 南京理工大学学报（社会科学版），2001（03）：46-49.

[100] 庄绎传. 英汉翻译简明教程 [M]. 北京：外语教学与研究出版社，2002.

（另外还参考了 http：//tem. koolearn. com/；http：//www. mtizt. com/；http：//www. nytimes. com/；http：//www. qqenglish. com/bn/；http：//www. nytimes-se. com/；http：//news. iyuba. com/；http：//language. chinadaily. com. cn/；http：//www. putclub. com/book/story. php? id = 533；http：//www. langfly. com/a/20121120/211420. shtml；http：//www. toutiao. com/i6449477001932702221/；http：//www. bigear. cn/news-65-123176. html；http：//www. bigear. cn/news-65-123176. html；https：//www. yahoo. com/news/bartomeu-says-messis-contract-signed-father-105319448-sow. html；http：//www. sohu. com/a/196645633_642305；http：//edu. sina. com. cn/zl/oversea/2017－07－12/doc－ifyhwefp0620932. shtml；http：//www. langfly. com/a/20100608/181450. shtml；http：//www. kekenet. com/read/201709/523972. shtml；https：//www. hjenglish. com/speeches/p1208365/；http：//www. lawinfochina. com/display. aspx? lib = dbref&id = 58；http：//kaoyan. xdf. cn/201603/10445803. html；http：//www. bigear. cn/news-65-123269. html；http：//www. china. org. cn/chinese/catl/2017-03/17/content _ 40498347. htm；http：//www. kekenet. com/kaoyan/201302/227467. shtml；https：//wenku. baidu. com/view/6888be7dbd64783e09122b7b. html；https：//max. book118. com/html/2015/0428/15968784. shtm；http：//www. tingclass. net/show-8694-395564-1. html；https：//wenku. baidu. com/view/21d6c69565ce0508763213d7. html；http：//www. putclub. com/html/ability/Forliteratures/20141231/94873. html）